Morphing Minds

Morphing Minds

Shaping Realities

Alina Hazel

Mohammed Altaf Hussain

CONTENTS

INDEX

6.2 Discuss psychological strategies for embracing change and fostering personal growth

6.3 Explore the concept of resilience and adaptability in morphing minds

Chapter 7: Mindful Practices for Reality Shaping

7.1 Introduce mindfulness and meditation as tools for mind morphing

7.2 Discuss the benefits of mindfulness in reducing stress and enhancing cognitive flexibility

7.3 Provide guided exercises for incorporating mindfulness into daily life

Chapter 8: Ethical Considerations in Reality Shaping

8.1 Explore the ethical implications of influencing personal and collective realities

8.2 Discuss the responsibility that comes with the power of shaping minds

8.3 Analyze the potential for positive and negative consequences in reality morphing

Chapter 9: The Future of Morphing Minds

9.1 Speculate on the future of mind morphing and reality shaping

9.2 Discuss emerging technologies and their potential impact on consciousness

9.3 Explore the evolving understanding of the mind and its role in shaping the future

Conclusion

Chapter 1

Introduction

In the many-sided embroidery of human life, the transaction between the psyche and the truth is a powerful power that has enraptured masterminds, researchers, and savants across ages. The human psyche, with its surprising limit with regards to creative mind, comprehension, and development, fills in as a pot where thoughts are produced, convictions are formed, and truths are shaped. The cooperative connection between the brain and the truth is a captivating landscape that coaxes investigation, and it is inside this setting that we leave on an excursion to disentangle the significant associations exemplified in the subject of "Transforming Psyches, Forming Real factors."

At the core of this investigation lies the central reason that the human brain isn't just a uninvolved onlooker of the world yet a functioning specialist equipped for trim and reshaping the actual texture of the real world. This idea rises above the customary limits of brain research and reasoning, diving into the domains of science, craftsmanship, culture, and innovation. It is a multi-faceted embroidery woven by the complicated strings of insight, discernment, innovativeness, and cultural elements, where the psyche's groundbreaking potential turns into an impetus for the development of our general surroundings.

To get a handle on the substance of this perplexing interaction, we should initially dive into the overly complex passages of the human psyche. The brain, a mysterious domain, is a nexus of considerations, feelings, recollections, and cognizance. It is inside this cauldron that discernments are conceived, thoughts flourish, and standards are built. The psyche, in its limitless intricacy, holds the ability to shape individual encounters as well as aggregate real factors. From the significant effect of conviction frameworks on social stories to the groundbreaking impact of imagination on cultural standards, the brain arises as a powerful power in the stupendous embroidery of human life.

As we explore the scene of transforming minds, we experience the many-sided dance among discernment and reality. Discernment, frequently viewed as an emotional focal point through which people decipher the world, turns into a key part during the time spent molding real factors. The brain's capacity to channel, decipher, and develop importance from tangible information establishes the groundwork for the different embroidery of human encounters. In this exchange among discernment and reality, we witness the rise of mental predispositions, social points of view, and individual mannerisms that on the whole add to the kaleidoscope of human insight.

The forming of real factors stretches out past the singular domain to envelop the shared mindset of social orders. Social structures, conviction frameworks, and cultural standards are not inconsistent builds but rather appearances of aggregate personalities at work. The intergenerational transmission of thoughts, values, and customs turns into a conductor through which the brain sustains its effect on the more extensive material of the real world. The transforming of aggregate personalities, appeared in social development, cultural changes, and authentic movements, divulges the multifaceted elements through which human social orders shape and reshape their real factors.

In the steadily developing scene of transforming minds, the job of imagination arises as a groundbreaking power that rises above ordinary limits. Imagination, a sign of the brain's ability to enhance and imagine additional opportunities, turns into an impetus for molding real factors in different spaces. From the imaginative articulations that reclassify stylish standards to the mechanical developments that change ventures, innovativeness fills in as a scaffold between the domain of thoughts and the substantial texture of the real world. It is from the perspective of innovativeness that we witness the significant effect of individual personalities on the aggregate woven artwork of human advancement.

Mechanical progressions, a sign of human creativity, epitomize the groundbreaking force of transforming minds in the domain of the real world. The direction of mechanical advancement is complicatedly connected to the creative limits of the human brain. From the creation of the wheel that reformed transportation to the computerized insurgency that reshaped correspondence, innovation turns into an unmistakable articulation of the brain's capacity to shape and reshape the outer world.

The crossing point of transforming minds and mechanical advancement opens new wildernesses, leading to moral predicaments, cultural changes, and exceptional potential outcomes.

The topic of transforming minds, molding real factors, resounds not just in that frame of mind of science and innovation yet additionally in the domain of cultural elements and social development. The aggregate mentality of social orders, set apart by shared values, belief systems, and goals, goes through persistent transformation. The recurring pattern of cultural mentalities towards issues like correspondence, equity, and common freedoms mirror the developing idea of aggregate personalities.

The transaction between individual convictions and cultural designs turns into a pot where cultural truths are fashioned and reclassified.

At the convergence of transforming brains and forming real factors, the impact of training turns into a urgent part of thought. The schooling systems intended to bestow information, impart values, and sustain decisive reasoning assume a urgent part in significantly shaping the personalities that, thusly, add to the aggregate development of real factors. The educational programs, academic methodologies, and instructive ways of thinking become instrumental in developing personalities that are educated as well as outfitted with the ability to address, enhance, and add to the continuous story of human advancement.

In the contemporary period, the computerized scene arises as a unique field where transforming minds apply a significant effect on the molding of augmented realities. The coming of the web, online entertainment, and virtual spaces intensifies the interconnectedness of brains across the globe. The trading of thoughts, the dispersal of data, and the arrangement of online networks become basic parts in the consistently growing embroidery of transforming minds. The computerized domain, with its uncommon speed and reach, acquaints new aspects with the manners by which minds on the whole shape the stories of the advanced age.

As we explore the complicated landscape of transforming brains and molding real factors, the moral components of this transaction come to the very front. The decisions made by people and social orders during the time spent forming real factors convey moral ramifications that reverberate across ages. The moral obligation inborn in the extraordinary force of the psyche requires an intelligent commitment with the outcomes of our aggregate activities. Issues like natural maintainability, civil rights, and moral contemplations in mechanical progressions highlight the basic for a moral compass in the excursion of transforming minds.

All in all, the subject of "Transforming Brains, Forming Real factors" welcomes us to set out on a significant investigation of the multifaceted exchange between the human psyche and the outer world. From the forming of individual discernments to the aggregate development of cultural real factors, the excursion unfurls in different aspects that navigate the domains of brain research, reasoning, science, craftsmanship, and innovation.

The embroidery of transforming minds is woven with the strings of imagination, discernment, social development, and mechanical advancement, offering an all encompassing perspective on the diverse manners by which the brain impacts and shapes the texture of the real world. As we explore this far reaching scene, the moral contemplations implanted in the groundbreaking force of the psyche highlight the basic for a smart and upright way to deal with the continuous course of molding real factors. In the sections that follow, we dive further into the complexities of explicit areas, investigating the extraordinary capability of transforming minds in the domains of science, workmanship, culture, innovation, and then some.

1.1 Introduce the concept of morphing minds and shaping realities

In the complicated dance between discernment, perception, and the outer world, the idea of "Transforming Psyches, Molding Real factors" arises as a charming investigation into the significant transaction between the human brain and the development of the world we possess. This subject exemplifies the unique relationship wherein the human brain, with its exceptional limit with regards to inventiveness, development, and insight, turns into an impetus for the trim and reshaping of the complicated texture of the real world. It welcomes us to dig into the profundities of the psyche's groundbreaking potential and its noteworthy effect on the outside world.

At the center of this investigation lies the acknowledgment that the human psyche is definitely not a detached beneficiary of reality however a functioning specialist that partakes in the persistent course of molding and reshaping our general surroundings. This idea rises above disciplinary limits, winding through the domains of brain research, reasoning, science, craftsmanship, culture, and innovation. It is a multi-faceted focal point through which we can look at the complicated strings associating the mental cycles inside the brain to the substantial signs in the outer world.

To understand the quintessence of transforming brains and forming real factors, it is basic to wander into the complicated scene of the human psyche itself. The brain, a cryptic and complex substance, fills in as the locus where considerations, feelings, recollections, and awareness meet. Inside this cauldron, discernments are framed, thoughts flourish, and the groundworks of conviction frameworks are laid. The psyche is certainly not a static element; it develops, adjusts, and answers improvements, forming individual encounters as well as the aggregate reality we share.

The exchange among discernment and the truth is a focal subject in understanding how transforming minds add to molding outer real factors. Discernment, frequently saw as an emotional channel through which people decipher the world, turns into a vital power in this unique relationship. The psyche's capacity to process, decipher, and relegate significance to tangible information shapes the reason for the assorted cluster of human encounters. In this transaction, mental predispositions, social points of view, and individual subtleties come to the front, aggregately adding to the kaleidoscope of human discernment.

The impact of transforming minds reaches out past the person to envelop the shared awareness of social orders. Social structures, conviction frameworks, and cultural standards are not erratic builds but rather impressions of aggregate personalities at work. The transmission of thoughts, values, and customs across ages turns into a conductor through which the psyche sustains its effect on the more extensive material of the real world. The transforming of aggregate personalities, as confirmed in social development, cultural changes, and verifiable movements, reveals the unpredictable elements through which human social orders shape and reshape their real factors over the long haul.

Imagination arises as an extraordinary power that rises above conventional limits and assumes an essential part during the time spent transforming psyches and molding real factors. Innovativeness, a statement of the psyche's ability to develop and imagine additional opportunities, fills in as an extension between the theoretical domain of thoughts and the unmistakable texture of the real world. It envelops creative undertakings that rethink stylish standards, logical forward leaps that reshape how we might interpret the world, and mechanical developments that alter ventures. From the perspective of imagination, we witness the significant effect of individual personalities on the aggregate woven artwork of human advancement.

Mechanical headways, a demonstration of human resourcefulness, epitomize the groundbreaking force of transforming minds in the domain of the real world. The direction of innovative advancement is unpredictably connected to the imaginative limits of the human brain. From old devices that upset work to contemporary computerized innovations that rethink correspondence, innovation turns into a substantial articulation of the psyche's capacity to shape and reshape the outside world. The crossing point of transforming minds and mechanical development opens new boondocks, bringing about moral issues, cultural changes, and remarkable conceivable outcomes.

The subject of transforming minds, molding real factors, resounds not just in that frame of mind of science and innovation yet in addition in cultural elements and social advancement. The aggregate outlook of social orders, set apart by shared values, belief systems, and goals, goes through nonstop transformation. The back and forth movement of cultural mentalities towards issues like uniformity, equity, and basic freedoms mirror the advancing idea of aggregate personalities. The interaction between individual convictions and cultural designs turns into a pot where cultural truths are manufactured and re-imagined.

In the contemporary time, the computerized scene arises as a unique field where transforming minds apply a significant effect on the forming of augmented realities. The appearance of the web, online entertainment, and virtual spaces intensifies the interconnectedness of brains across the globe.

The trading of thoughts, the scattering of data, and the arrangement of online networks become vital parts in the steadily extending embroidered artwork of transforming minds. The computerized domain, with its phenomenal speed and reach, acquaints new aspects with the manners by which minds aggregately shape the accounts of the advanced age.

Schooling arises as a crucial perspective in the exchange between transforming brains and forming real factors. School systems, intended to confer information, impart values, and sustain decisive reasoning, assume an essential part in shaping the personalities that add to the aggregate development of real factors. The educational programs, academic methodologies, and instructive ways of thinking become instrumental in developing personalities that are educated as well as furnished with the ability to address, improve, and add to the continuous story of human advancement.

As we explore the perplexing territory of transforming psyches and forming real factors, the moral elements of this transaction come to the front. The decisions made by people and social orders during the time spent molding real factors convey moral ramifications that reverberate across ages. Issues like natural supportability, civil rights, and moral contemplations in mechanical progressions highlight the basic for a moral compass in the excursion of transforming minds.

All in all, the subject of "Transforming Brains, Molding Real factors" welcomes us to leave on a significant investigation of the many-sided transaction between the human psyche and the outer world. From the forming of individual discernments to the aggregate development of cultural real factors, the excursion unfurls in different aspects that cross the domains of brain research, reasoning, science, craftsmanship, and innovation. The embroidery of transforming minds is woven with the strings of imagination, discernment, social development, and mechanical advancement, offering an all encompassing perspective on the diverse manners by which the psyche impacts and shapes the texture of the real world. As we explore this broad scene, the moral contemplations implanted in the groundbreaking force of the brain highlight the basic for a smart and honest way to deal with the continuous course of molding real factors.

1.2 Explore the interconnected nature of thoughts, beliefs, and the external world

In the perplexing dance of human cognizance, the interconnected idea of contemplations, convictions, and the outer world winds around an embroidery that shapes our impression of the real world. This perplexing exchange is a basic part of the human experience, digging into the domains of brain science, reasoning, and neuroscience. Understanding how contemplations and convictions impact our collaboration with the outside world requires a nuanced investigation of mental cycles, conviction frameworks, and the powerful idea of discernment.

At the core of this investigation is the idea that our contemplations, the psychological builds that emerge to us, are not disengaged elements but rather interconnected strings that weave the texture of our awareness. Considerations are not simple brief events; they are the structure blocks of comprehension, addressing the powerful interaction of neurons, neurotransmitters, and synapses inside the perplexing design of the cerebrum. As considerations arise and interlace, they bring about examples of perception that shape how we might interpret the world.

Convictions, firmly lined up with contemplations, apply a significant impact on the manner in which we decipher and draw in with the outside world. Convictions are the mental designs that mirror our convictions, values, and presumptions about the real world. They act as focal points through which we channel data, simply decide, and explore the intricacies of our environmental elements. Convictions are not static;

they advance, adjust, and are affected by the ceaseless transaction between our inward mental scene and the outside improvements that shape our encounters.

The unique connection between considerations, convictions, and the outside world turns out to be especially clear in the domain of discernment. Discernment is certainly not a latent gathering of tangible data; rather, it is a functioning and interpretative cycle formed by the mind boggling interchange of mental cycles. The psyche, in its unending undertaking to get a handle on the world, channels, coordinates, and relegates significance to tangible info. This cycle is intensely impacted by our viewpoints and convictions, which go about as channels that variety our discernments and add to the development of our emotional reality.

Mental predispositions, innate propensities in the manner in which we process data, assume a huge part in shaping our contemplations, convictions, and at last, our view of the outer world. These predispositions, going from tendency to look for predictable feedback to the accessibility heuristic, influence our dynamic cycles and add to the arrangement and support of convictions. The interconnected idea of contemplations and convictions subsequently stretches out past the individual, affecting the aggregate mentality of social orders, societies, and networks.

The social component of convictions features the common idea of mental systems inside networks. Shared convictions structure the reason for social stories, cultural standards, and aggregate characters. The interaction between individual convictions and cultural develops makes an input circle wherein the aggregate outlook supports and shapes the convictions of people, as well as the other way around. This unpredictable dance between the individual and the aggregate highlights the interconnected idea of contemplations and convictions in forming the more extensive real factors of human social orders.

Looking at the interconnected idea of contemplations, convictions, and the outer world likewise requires digging into the philosophical elements of epistemology and metaphysics. Epistemology, the investigation of information, investigates how we come to be aware and figure out the world.

Philosophy, then again, digs into the idea of reality itself. The transaction between these philosophical domains is integral to appreciating how our contemplations and convictions add to how we might interpret reality.

According to an epistemological viewpoint, our contemplations are basic to the most common way of knowing. Whether through experimental perception, thinking, or instinct, our mental resources are participated in the consistent quest for information. Nonetheless, the subjectivity innate in individual contemplations and convictions acquaints a layer of intricacy with the topic of how we come to be aware. The focal point through which we see the world is molded by our mental cycles, impacting the procurement and understanding of information.

Ontologically, the idea of the truth is complicatedly attached to our convictions about presence, being, and the outside world. Different philosophical and social customs offer assorted ontological systems that shape how we might interpret reality. Whether established in strict cosmologies, logical ideal models, or existential methods of reasoning, our convictions about the idea of reality impact the manner in which we see and draw in with the outside world. The interconnected idea of considerations and convictions, consequently, stretches out past the mental domain to add to the ontological groundworks of our common reality.

The pliability of convictions and the pliancy of the human brain present the idea of mental adaptability — a vital viewpoint in the interconnected idea of contemplations, convictions, and the outer world. Mental adaptability alludes to the capacity to adjust and change one's considerations and convictions in light of new data or evolving conditions. A powerful part of perception permits people to explore the intricacies of the outside world by integrating clever thoughts, testing existing convictions, and embracing a more nuanced comprehension of the real world.

Mental firmness, alternately, can prompt mental unbending nature, where people stick to laid out convictions in spite of problematic proof. This inflexibility can ruin the ability to adjust to new data, obstructing self-improvement, and restricting the capacity to develop a more precise and nuanced view of the outside world. The investigation of mental adaptability and resoluteness discloses the significant ramifications of the interconnected idea of considerations and convictions on individual insight and, likewise, cultural elements.

The exchange between considerations, convictions, and the outer world is likewise appeared in the peculiarity of unavoidable outcomes. An unavoidable outcome happens when a conviction or assumption impacts conduct such that makes the conviction work out as expected. This recurrent interaction exhibits how contemplations and convictions, when assimilated and followed up on, can shape the outer world and support the very convictions that started the cycle. Whether in private connections, instructive settings, or cultural designs, unavoidable outcomes highlight the force of convictions in affecting the real factors we make.

In the domain of neuroscience, the investigation of brain adaptability further enlightens the interconnected idea of considerations, convictions, and the outside world. Brain adaptability alludes to the mind's capacity to revamp itself by framing new brain associations over the course of life. This unique interaction is affected by encounters, learning, and ecological elements. The considerations we participate in, the convictions we hold, and the outside upgrades we experience add to the chiseling of brain connections, mirroring the continuous dance between the psyche and the outer world inside the multifaceted scene of the cerebrum.

The interconnection among contemplations and feelings adds one more layer of intricacy to the investigation of mental cycles and their effect on the outer world. Feelings, unpredictably attached to our viewpoints and convictions, assume an essential part in forming our reactions to the outer climate. The entwined idea of considerations and feelings adds to the extravagance and profundity of human experience, affecting our insights, choices, and connections with our general surroundings.

Investigating the interconnected idea of contemplations, convictions, and the outside world likewise requires an assessment of the job of language in forming mental systems. Language, as a vehicle for offering viewpoints and imparting convictions, turns into an instrument through which people develop and convey how they might interpret reality. The semantic portrayals of contemplations and convictions add to the social component of discernment, cultivating shared accounts, social talk, and the transmission of information across ages.

With regards to the interconnected idea of considerations and the outer world, care rehearses offer an interesting viewpoint. Care includes developing an attention to one's viewpoints and encounters right now without judgment. By noticing contemplations and feelings without connection, people can foster an elevated aversion to the manners by which their interior mental cycles impact their impression of the outer world. Care rehearses, established in pondering customs, feature the groundbreaking capability of deliberately captivating with the interconnected idea of considerations and the outside world.

The ramifications of the interconnected idea of contemplations, convictions, and the outside world reach out into the domains of direction, critical thinking, and inventiveness. Navigation, impacted by mental cycles and conviction frameworks, shapes the direction of individual lives and cultural turns of events. The exchange among considerations and convictions turns out to be especially obvious in basic choice focuses, where mental predispositions, heuristics, and the impact of cultural standards merge to affect individuals decisions.

Critical thinking, as a mental undertaking, depends on the interconnected idea of considerations to create inventive arrangements. The capacity to interface different snippets of data, think basically, and consider elective viewpoints is impacted by the adaptability and versatility of mental cycles.

The investigation of interconnected contemplations with regards to critical thinking highlights the significance of mental variety and receptiveness in cultivating effective fixes to complex difficulties.

Inventiveness, as a sign of the interconnected idea of considerations and convictions, depends on the capacity to cross flighty mental pathways. Inventive undertakings frequently include splitting away from laid out thought designs, testing existing convictions, and investigating novel points of view. The pliability of convictions and the limit with regards to mental adaptability assume a focal part in the innovative flow, permitting people to rise above regular limits and add to the development of social, creative, and logical scenes.

All in all, the investigation of the interconnected idea of considerations, convictions, and the outside world reveals a rich embroidery that shapes our view of the real world. From the mental cycles inside the mind to the cultural builds that impact aggregate convictions, the transaction among contemplations and the outside world is a dynamic and complex peculiarity. Understanding this interconnectedness is essential for exploring the intricacies of human experience, encouraging mental adaptability, and developing a more nuanced and versatile commitment with the consistently changing outside climate. As we dig into the complexities of this exchange, we gain experiences into the groundbreaking capability of contemplations and convictions in significantly shaping individual lives, cultural elements, and the developing stories of human life.

1.3 Discuss the power of perception in influencing personal and collective realities

Discernment, the multifaceted cycle through which people decipher and get a handle on the world, holds a significant impact in molding both individual and aggregate real factors. This power radiates from the human psyche's capacity to develop importance from tactile information, an interaction that is profoundly laced with mental, close to home, and social elements. Understanding the elements of discernment permits us to unwind the intricacies of how people see their own world and add to the development of shared cultural accounts.

At its center, discernment is an emotional encounter, impacted by a singular's interesting mental cycles, close to home states, and previous encounters. The psyche, going about as a channel for tangible data, coordinates and deciphers information from the outside climate, leading to individualized insights. This subjectivity acquaints a layer of intricacy with the thought of the real world, as every individual's understanding of similar situation can shift essentially.

Mental cycles assume a vital part in the force of discernment. The cerebrum, with its complicated brain organizations, processes and coordinates tangible contribution to make a reasonable portrayal of the outer world. Mental predispositions, intrinsic propensities in data handling, shape the manner in which people channel and decipher information.

From tendency to look for predetermined feedback, where individuals will generally look for data that affirms their previous convictions, to the radiance impact, where one trademark impacts the general impression of an individual or circumstance, these inclinations add to the embellishment of individual real factors.

Feelings further variety the focal point through which people see the world. Close to home states impact the translation of occasions, forming the generally profound tone of one's existence. For example, a positive profound state might prompt more hopeful understandings of circumstances, while a pessimistic close to home state can add to a more critical viewpoint. The interconnected idea of comprehension and feeling highlights the complexities of discernment and its job in forming individual real factors.

The social and social setting wherein people exist adds one more layer to the force of insight. Social standards, cultural assumptions, and shared convictions on the whole add to the development of an aggregate reality. People, affected by the social milieu in which they are implanted, take on specific perceptual systems that line up with the overall standards of their general public. This common discernment adds to the development of aggregate stories that shape the personality and perspective of whole networks.

The idea of social development of the real world, as expressed by sociologists Berger and Luckmann, features how society by and large makes and keeps a mutual perspective of the world. This cycle includes the externalization of shared implications through language, the generalization of these implications in friendly organizations, and the assimilation of these implications by people, molding their view of the real world. Along these lines, the force of discernment turns into a social peculiarity, with aggregate convictions impacting the development of a common reality.

Media, as a strong force to be reckoned with of discernment, assumes a huge part in molding aggregate real factors. The pictures, accounts, and data scattered through different media channels add to the development of cultural standards, values, and mentalities. Media reflects as well as shapes social stories, impacting popular assessment and adding to the arrangement of aggregate discernments. The effect of media on discernment turns out to be especially obvious in issues of portrayal, where the depiction of specific gatherings or occasions can impact public mentalities and add to the forming of cultural real factors.

The force of discernment is apparent in the arrangement of generalizations and biases, which frequently emerge from mental alternate ways and social order. Generalizations, misrepresented and summed up convictions about a specific gathering, impact how people see and interface with others. These assumptions, profoundly implanted in cultural cognizance, can add to unfair ways of behaving and shape the social elements inside a local area. The force of discernment in encouraging or testing generalizations has sweeping ramifications for cultivating inclusivity and advancing social union.

In the domain of brain research, the idea of diagram hypothesis gives bits of knowledge into how prior mental structures impact the understanding of new data. Blueprints are mental designs that coordinate information and guide data handling. They are created through experience and add to the productivity of mental cycles. Notwithstanding, when people depend too vigorously on existing mappings, it can prompt specific consideration and translation, building up assumptions and restricting the capacity to see elective viewpoints.

The job of discernment in affecting individual and aggregate real factors turns out to be especially striking with regards to political and philosophical convictions. People frequently channel data from the perspective of their political affiliations, prompting one-sided translations of occasions and issues. The peculiarity of spurred thinking, where people specifically process data to line up with their previous convictions, further highlights the force of discernment in molding political real factors. The enraptured idea of public talk, driven by unique impression of similar arrangement of realities, epitomizes how profoundly dug in convictions can impact aggregate real factors.

The force of discernment stretches out past the mental and close to home domains to affect physiological reactions. A self-influenced consequence, for example, shows the way that the confidence in the viability of a treatment can prompt real physiological upgrades, even without a trace of dynamic fixings. This brain body association features the many-sided transaction between mental states and actual prosperity, stressing the job of discernment in affecting wellbeing results.

In the domain of neuroscience, research on brain adaptability reveals insight into the mind's capacity to rearrange itself in light of involvement and discernment. The brain processes that underlie discernment can be molded and adjusted through learning and openness to new encounters. This pliancy of the mind supports that discernments are not fixed yet can be moldable, giving roads to self-awareness and change.

The idea of perceptual learning further underlines the unique idea of discernment. Through openness to new improvements and encounters, people can refine and upgrade their perceptual abilities. This interaction includes both base up handling, where tangible data adds to the development of insights, and hierarchical handling, where existing information and assumptions shape the translation of tactile information. Perceptual learning features the flexibility of discernment and its part in gaining skill in unambiguous spaces.

The ramifications of the force of insight stretch out to fields like training, where how data is introduced can impact understudies' comprehension and maintenance. Instructive conditions that encourage a positive and comprehensive climate add to a more valuable impression of getting the hang of, advancing commitment and scholarly achievement. The plan of opportunities for growth, considering the force of insight, can essentially affect the instructive results and the advancement of mental abilities.

In the domain of relational connections, the force of discernment is apparent in the arrangement of social securities and the elements of correspondence. The manner in which people see each other impacts the nature of connections and communications. Miscommunications and clashes frequently emerge from varying discernments, underscoring the requirement for viable correspondence and sympathetic comprehension to connect perceptual holes.

The force of insight isn't bound to the singular level however stretches out to the cultural level, where aggregate discernments shape the stories that characterize a local area or country. Verifiable occasions, for instance, are dependent upon understanding, and the aggregate memory of a general public is molded by how these occasions are seen and recalled. The contestation of verifiable stories highlights the complicated interchange between power, memory, and the development of aggregate real factors.

The investigation of the force of discernment welcomes reflection on how people and social orders can encourage a more nuanced and receptive way to deal with figuring out the world. Care rehearses, which urge people to develop consciousness of their viewpoints and insights, offer a pathway to breaking constant idea designs and advancing mental adaptability. The affirmation of the subjectivity of insight makes the way for compassion, as people perceive that others might have unique however similarly legitimate viewpoints.

All in all, the force of discernment in impacting individual and aggregate truths is a complex peculiarity that envelops mental, profound, social, and social aspects. From the person's mental cycles and close to home states to the cultural develops that shape aggregate convictions, the interaction among discernment and the truth is dynamic and complex. Understanding the force of discernment gives experiences into the arrangement of individual convictions, the elements of relational connections, and the development of shared cultural stories. By recognizing the subjectivity of discernment and cultivating mental adaptability, people and social orders can explore the complexities of the human involvement in more prominent sympathy, receptiveness, and an appreciation for the assorted manners by which the truth is seen.

The impact of individual and aggregate truths is a dynamic and complicated interaction between individual discernments, cultural develops, and shared encounters. Understanding how these powers shape how we might interpret the world requires an investigation of mental, social, and social aspects. The ability to impact individual and aggregate real factors lies in the mental cycles of people as well as in the more extensive stories and designs that characterize social orders.

At the singular level, insight fills in as the focal point through which the truth is built. The brain, a mind boggling organization of mental cycles and tangible encounters, deciphers and cycles data from the outside climate to make an emotional comprehension of the real world. This subjectivity presents fluctuation in how people see and decipher similar situation, prompting different individual real factors.

Mental cycles, like consideration, memory, and thinking, assume a crucial part in molding individual real factors. Consideration figures out which improvements are featured and handled, impacting what data becomes remarkable in a singular's discernment. Memory, formed by previous encounters and feelings, adds to the development of a story that illuminates present discernments. Thinking, impacted by mental predispositions and heuristics, guides people in figuring out the world, frequently prompting thought processes that shape individual real factors.

Feelings, entwined with mental cycles, add a layer of intricacy to individual insights. Close to home states impact the understanding of occasions, shading the in general profound tone of one's existence. Positive feelings might prompt more hopeful translations, while gloomy feelings can add to a more cynical standpoint. The transaction among comprehension and feeling highlights the profoundly coordinated nature of the human experience and the diverse manners by which individual truths are developed.

The cultural component of individual truths is obvious in the social development of reality hypothesis. This viewpoint, spearheaded by sociologists Berger and Luckmann, sets that the truth is definitely not a goal, outer element however is socially developed through shared implications and translations. Language, social establishments, and social practices act as devices through which people externalize, typify, and incorporate shared implications, adding to the development of individual real factors inside the more extensive cultural setting.

Media, as a strong specialist in forming discernments, assumes a critical part in the social development of the real world. The pictures, stories, and data scattered through different media channels add to the formation of cultural standards, values, and mentalities. Media reflects as well as shapes social stories, affecting popular assessment and adding to the development of aggregate insights. The effect of media on private and aggregate real factors turns out to be especially articulated in issues of portrayal, where the depiction of specific gatherings or occasions impacts public mentalities and shapes cultural real factors.

The ability to impact individual and aggregate truths is additionally manifest in the arrangement of generalizations and biases. These mental alternate ways and social classifications impact how people see and interface with others. Generalizations, misrepresented and summed up convictions about a specific gathering, shape the manner in which people approach social circumstances, adding to the development of individual and aggregate real factors. Biases, established in these generalizations, can prompt oppressive ways of behaving and influence social elements.

Schooling, as a cultural foundation, assumes a huge part in forming individual and aggregate real factors. The educational program, academic methodologies, and social stories inside schooling systems add to the development of information and values. The instructive climate, incorporating communications with friends and teachers, impacts the advancement of mental structures, convictions, and insights.

As people travel through instructive foundations, their own truths are constantly molded by the data, values, and viewpoints bestowed by the school system.

Political and philosophical convictions are strong powerhouses of individual and aggregate real factors. People frequently channel data from the perspective of their political affiliations, prompting one-sided understandings of occasions and issues. The peculiarity of roused thinking, where people specifically process data to line up with their previous convictions, highlights the force of philosophical systems in molding individual and aggregate real factors. The spellbound idea of public talk, driven by unique view of similar arrangement of realities, represents how profoundly settled in convictions can impact cultural real factors.

Authentic stories, molded by aggregate memory and cultural translations of the past, add to the development of shared real factors. How verifiable occasions are seen and recollected impacts the aggregate character of a local area or country. The contestation of verifiable accounts highlights the complicated interaction between power, memory, and the development of individual and aggregate real factors. Cultural accounts about the past shape how people comprehend history as well as illuminate their present and future points of view.

The force of discernment to impact individual and aggregate real factors stretches out past mental and profound domains to affect physiological reactions. A self-influenced consequence, for example, shows the way that the confidence in the viability of a treatment can prompt genuine physiological upgrades, even without any dynamic fixings. This brain body association features the perplexing transaction between mental states and actual prosperity, underlining the job of discernment in affecting wellbeing results.

Neuroscience research on brain adaptability reveals insight into the mind's capacity to rearrange itself in light of involvement and discernment. The brain connections that underlie insight can be molded and altered through learning and openness to new encounters. This versatility of the mind supports that discernments are not fixed however can be pliable, giving roads to self-awareness and change.

The idea of perceptual learning further accentuates the unique idea of insight. Through openness to new boosts and encounters, people can refine and improve their perceptual abilities. This cycle includes both base up handling, where tactile data adds to the development of insights, and hierarchical handling, where existing information and assumptions shape the understanding of tangible information. Perceptual learning features the flexibility of discernment and its job in securing aptitude in unambiguous areas.

Care rehearses, which urge people to develop familiarity with their viewpoints and discernments, offer a pathway to breaking routine idea designs and advancing mental adaptability.

The act of care includes non-critical perception of considerations and sensations, encouraging an uplifted aversion to the manners by which inner mental cycles impact impression of the outside world. By developing care, people can foster a more nuanced and liberal way to deal with grasping individual and aggregate real factors.

All in all, the ability to impact individual and aggregate truths is a diverse peculiarity that envelops mental, close to home, social, and social aspects. From the person's mental cycles and profound states to the more extensive cultural builds that shape aggregate convictions, the transaction among discernment and the truth is dynamic and complex. Perceiving the subjectivity of insight makes the way for sympathy, as people comprehend that others might have unique yet similarly substantial points of view. By recognizing the unpredictable interchange among individual and aggregate real factors, social orders can encourage a more nuanced, receptive, and sympathetic way to deal with exploring the intricacies of the human experience.

Chapter 2

The Power of Mind Morphing

In the immense scene of human potential, the brain remains as a strange region, a domain of endless conceivable outcomes ready to be investigated and tackled. The idea of brain transforming, a groundbreaking interaction that opens the inactive capacities of the human psyche, has enraptured the creative mind of masterminds, logicians, and researchers all through the ages. This investigation digs into the significant profundities of brain transforming, following its underlying foundations, grasping its systems, and pondering its suggestions for the fate of humankind.

At the core of psyche transforming lies the conundrum of awareness. The subtle power characterizes our reality, giving an emotional encounter to our generally true reality. The journey to comprehend cognizance has been an interminable undertaking, with researchers and spiritualists the same looking to disentangle its secrets. Mind transforming, generally, is a cognizant work to reshape, grow, and refine the forms of one's psychological scene.

The excursion into the domain of psyche transforming starts with an affirmation of the pliancy of the cerebrum. Brain adaptability, the cerebrum's capacity to revamp itself by shaping new brain associations over the course of life, is a foundation of psyche transforming. This unique nature of the cerebrum challenges the well established conviction that its design is unbending and unchanging. All things being equal, it recommends that the psyche is a flexible element, equipped for variation and change.

The force of psyche transforming stretches out past simple mental improvement; it includes the comprehensive advancement of the person. This change includes scholarly resources as well as the capacity to appreciate people on a deeper level, imagination, and, surprisingly, otherworldly mindfulness. The reconciliation of these features results in an agreeable and engaged individual, equipped for exploring the intricacies of presence with effortlessness and versatility.

To grasp the capability of psyche transforming, one should investigate the crossing point of antiquated insight and present day science. Over the entire course of time, different scrutinizing customs have perceived the extraordinary force of the psyche. Practices like reflection, care, and perception have been fundamental to these customs, offering people a way to investigate the profundities of their cognizance.

In late many years, logical exploration has approved a considerable lot of these old works on, revealing insight into the neurobiological systems that underlie mind transforming. Concentrates on care reflection, for example, have shown changes in mind construction and capability, featuring the unmistakable effect of mental practices on the actual organ that houses awareness.

The cooperative energy between old insight and current science opens an entryway to another time of human potential. As innovation advances, instruments and strategies arise to work with mind transforming on phenomenal scales. Mind machine interfaces, neurofeedback gadgets, and augmented reality stages are among the state of the art advances that guarantee to intensify our mental capacities and reshape the manner in which we see and associate with the world.

Be that as it may, to whom much is given, much will be expected. The moral ramifications of brain transforming request cautious thought. As we open the privileged insights of the psyche, questions emerge about the expected abuse of such information. Issues of security, assent, and the unseen side-effects of brain modifying intercessions loom not too far off. Society should wrestle with these moral scrapes to guarantee that psyche transforming serves the aggregate great instead of turning into an instrument for control or control.

The investigation of brain transforming likewise reaches out into the domain of human probability. What levels might the human mind at any point reach, and what limits, if any, compel its development? The idea of rising above human restrictions has been a repetitive topic in sci-fi and speculative way of thinking. As psyche transforming innovations advance, the possibility of upgrading insight, broadening life expectancy, and in any event, accomplishing a type of computerized everlasting status turns into a subject of sincere request.

The intermingling of man-made consciousness with mind transforming acquaints a captivating aspect with the talk. Could human awareness at any point be reproduced or even outperformed by counterfeit elements? The moral situations encompassing the formation of cognizant machines suggest significant conversation starters about the idea of awareness itself. As we adventure into the strange regions of psyche transforming, we should wrestle with the ramifications of playing gods in the domain of creation.

The cultural effect of psyche transforming is another aspect that requests examination. How might the change of individual personalities echo through the texture of networks and countries? Will it lead to more prominent amicability, understanding, and cooperation, or will it intensify existing divisions and imbalances? The democratization of psyche transforming advances brings up issues about openness and value, guaranteeing that the advantages of mental improvement are not bound to special elites.

Training, as a foundation of cultural turn of events, assumes a crucial part in forming the story of psyche transforming. Conventional instructive ideal models might have to develop to oblige the changing scene of human comprehension. Underlining information securing as well as the development of decisive reasoning, the ability to understand people on a profound level, and flexibility becomes central in planning people for the difficulties and valuable open doors that psyche transforming presents.

The entwining of psyche and profound quality arises as a focal topic in the talk on mind transforming. The improvement of upgraded mental capacities should be joined by a comparing moral structure that guides people in the mindful utilization of their freshly discovered powers. The deep rooted saying, "to whom much is given, much will be expected," resounds with recently discovered importance with regards to mind transforming.

Otherworldliness, frequently viewed as the domain of the extraordinary, additionally finds reverberation in the investigation of psyche transforming. Could the development of cognizance at any point prompt a more profound association with the otherworldly components of presence? The blend of science and otherworldliness opens roads for an all encompassing comprehension of the human experience, where the limits between the material and the supernatural haze.

The social and creative elements of psyche transforming add one more layer to its multi-layered investigation. How might the innovative articulations of people develop when their brains are freed from traditional limitations? The combination of innovation and imaginative undertakings might bring about new types of articulation, testing conventional thoughts of inventiveness and magnificence.

The stories encompassing brain transforming reach out past the individual and include shared awareness. The interconnectedness of psyches in a hyper-associated world raises the possibility of a worldwide brain, where shared contemplations and encounters rise above individual limits. The ramifications of such a shared perspective are significant, impacting the elements of participation, struggle, and the actual texture of human culture.

As we explore the strange waters of psyche transforming, the job of administration becomes significant. Administrative structures should be laid out to guarantee the moral turn of events and arrangement of brain adjusting innovations. Shields against abuse, security of individual independence, and the advancement of cultural prosperity ought to be essential parts of administrative designs intended to administer mind transforming.

The eventual fate of brain transforming is an embroidery woven with the strings of plausibility and vulnerability. The direction we decide to follow, as people and as a general public, will shape the forms of this unfurling story. The obligation to employ the force of brain transforming prudently falls upon the aggregate shoulders of mankind, encouraging us to graph a course that praises the pride of the individual, regards the interconnectedness, everything being equal, and explores the moral intricacies with shrewdness and sympathy.

Taking everything into account, the force of psyche transforming allures us to investigate the profundities of our cognizance, opening the idle potential that dwells inside. An excursion rises above the limits of science, reasoning, and otherworldliness, welcoming us to reclassify being human. As we stand on the slope of another period, the decisions in tackling the force of brain transforming will shape the predetermination of mankind for a long time into the future. The story of psyche transforming is as yet being composed, and every person, as their very own creator cognizance, contributes a special part to this unfurling epic.

2.1 Examine the neuroscience behind cognitive flexibility and adaptability

The many-sided dance of neurons inside the human mind organizes an orchestra of mental cycles, among which mental adaptability and versatility arise as central participants. To comprehend the neuroscience behind these intellectual capacities is to leave on an excursion into the brain engineering that empowers us to explore the steadily changing scene of our encounters, take care of intricate issues, and gain from novel circumstances.

At the center of mental adaptability lies the prefrontal cortex, a district of the cerebrum answerable for chief capabilities, for example, navigation, critical thinking, and working memory. This cerebrum force to be reckoned with coordinates data from different tangible modalities and organizes reactions that line up with our objectives and goals. The prefrontal cortex is certainly not a solid design; rather, it comprises of interconnected subregions, each adding to explicit parts of mental adaptability.

One such subregion is the dorsolateral prefrontal cortex (DLPFC), known for its part in working memory and mental control. It goes about as a focal center for organizing and incorporating data from other cerebrum locales, permitting us to deftly move between undertakings, viewpoints, and systems. Harm or brokenness in the DLPFC can prompt hindrances in mental adaptability, appearing as challenges in adjusting to new circumstances or changing plans on the fly.

One more critical player in the neuroscientific scene of mental adaptability is the foremost cingulate cortex (ACC). This locale is engaged with observing struggles, recognizing blunders, and changing way of behaving as needs be. It assumes a urgent part in the capacity to switch among undertakings and answer evolving requests. The ACC goes about as a sentinel, cautioning the cerebrum when changes are required and working with the redistribution of mental assets to upgrade execution.

The orbitofrontal cortex (OFC), arranged ventrally in the prefrontal cortex, adds to navigation and the assessment of remuneration and discipline. Its association in mental adaptability is clear in situations where people should adjust their decisions in view of changing prize possibilities. The OFC coordinates close to home and inspirational signs, adding a nuanced layer to the neurobiological underpinnings of versatile way of behaving.

While the prefrontal cortex becomes the overwhelming focus in the show of mental adaptability, its supporting cast incorporates an organization of interconnected mind locales. The striatum, a subcortical construction associated with remuneration handling and propensity development, teams up with the prefrontal cortex to work with objective coordinated conduct. The hippocampus, vital for memory development and spatial route, adds to our capacity to review and apply data from previous encounters deftly.

Synapses, the compound couriers that work with correspondence between neurons, assume a vital part in regulating mental adaptability. Dopamine, specifically, has been embroiled in remuneration based learning and the refreshing of activity result affiliations. The sensitive equilibrium of dopamine levels inside the prefrontal cortex and its interconnected areas impacts the cerebrum's capacity to adjust to changing conditions and gain from criticism.

The complicated exchange of these brain designs and synapse frameworks leads to the peculiarity of mental adaptability, permitting us to consistently move consideration, update mental portrayals, and change conduct in light of the always moving requests of our current circumstance. In any case, the story doesn't end here; the neuroscience of versatility dives significantly more profound into the systems that underlie our ability to gain for a fact and change our mental methodologies.

The idea of brain adaptability, the mind's capacity to redesign itself because of involvement, frames the underpinning of versatility. At the minute level, synaptic versatility — the reinforcing or debilitating of associations between neurons — underlies learning and memory. Long haul potentiation (LTP) and long haul wretchedness (LTD) are cell processes that mirror the fortifying or debilitating of synaptic associations, individually, and are key to versatile learning.

The hippocampus, a seahorse-formed structure settled profound inside the mind, is a brain adaptability area of interest. It assumes a critical part in the development of long winded recollections and spatial route, processes that add to our capacity to adjust to new conditions and gain from previous encounters. As we experience novel circumstances, the hippocampus works with the encoding of significant data, empowering us to recover and apply this information in comparable settings.

Past the hippocampus, the amygdala, an almond-formed group of cores, adds to profound learning and memory. Profound encounters convey a powerful effect on our versatile reactions, and the amygdala's contribution in partner feelings with boosts impacts our capacity to learn and adjust in light of the close to home meaning of occasions.

Synaptic versatility stretches out past the domains of memory development to shape the brain circuits that underlie direction and conduct. The striatum, a basic player in remuneration handling and propensity development, goes through synaptic versatility as we figure out how to connect explicit activities with positive or adverse results. This cycle adds to the development of propensities, robotizing certain ways of behaving to upgrade effectiveness in routine errands.

The synapse glutamate, a universal player in excitatory flagging, becomes the overwhelming focus in synaptic pliancy. The N-methyl-D-aspartate (NMDA) receptor, a kind of glutamate receptor, is crucial in the enlistment of LTP, working with the reinforcing of synaptic associations. The sensitive equilibrium of glutamate flagging directs the pliancy of brain circuits, chiseling the versatility of the mind because of involvement.

The job of neurotrophic factors, proteins that help the development and endurance of neurons, further highlights the versatile idea of the mind. Mind determined neurotrophic factor (BDNF), specifically, has accumulated consideration for its contribution in synaptic versatility, neuronal endurance, and the arrangement of new associations. BDNF goes about as a sub-atomic planner, molding the underlying and utilitarian scene of the mind in light of involvement.

The impact of hereditary qualities on mental adaptability and flexibility adds a layer of intricacy to the neuroscientific story. Hereditary varieties can affect the design and capability of key mind locales engaged with these cycles. For instance, polymorphisms in qualities connected with dopamine receptors or neurotrophic elements might impact a singular's inclination to mental adaptability and their ability for versatile learning.

Ecological variables, from early valuable encounters to progressing mental feeling, additionally add to the chiseling of brain circuits. The idea of involvement subordinate pliancy features how our cooperations with the climate, whether through mastering another ability or exploring social connections, shape the useful availability of the mind. The wealth of our encounters adds to the variety of versatile reactions showed by people.

The investigation of mental adaptability and flexibility has pragmatic ramifications for fields going from training to clinical brain research. In instructive settings, understanding the brain systems that underlie versatile learning can illuminate educational methodologies that upgrade understudies' capacity to embrace new ideas and apply information in different settings. Instructive mediations that exploit brain adaptability might offer novel ways to deal with encouraging mental adaptability in students.

In the domain of clinical brain research, experiences into the neuroscience of flexibility have suggestions for understanding and treating conditions described by unbending idea designs or impeded learning. Issues like over the top habitual problem (OCD), post-horrendous pressure problem (PTSD), and certain types of fixation might include dysregulation in the brain circuits that underlie mental adaptability. Designated mediations that address these brain components hold guarantee for further developing treatment results.

The ramifications of mental adaptability and versatility stretch out past the person to the aggregate elements of society. In a quickly impacting world, the capacity of networks and countries to adjust to new difficulties becomes central. Cultural designs that encourage development, liberality, and the free trade of thoughts add to the aggregate mental adaptability expected to explore the intricacies of the cutting edge time.

The convergence of neuroscience and man-made brainpower (computer based intelligence) acquaints an interesting aspect with the investigation of mental adaptability. As simulated intelligence frameworks become progressively complex, understanding the brain components that underlie human versatility can advise the improvement regarding simulated intelligence models that imitate parts of human perception. The journey to make simulated intelligence with mental adaptability opens roads for co-operative organizations among human and machine insight.

Be that as it may, as we dig into the neuroscience of mental adaptability and versatility, moral contemplations pose a potential threat. The possibility of controlling these brain components brings up issues about the capable utilization of neuroscientific information. Mental improvement intercessions, whether pharmacological or mechanical, require cautious moral examination to guarantee that they line up with standards of independence, equity, and the prosperity of people.

2.2 Explore case studies and examples of individuals who have transformed their lives through changing their mindset

The human psyche, with its astounding limit with regards to variation and change, has the ability to shape the course of one's life. Endless stories flourish of people who, through a significant change in outlook, have explored difficulties, beat impediments, and accomplished phenomenal self-improvement. Inspecting these contextual investigations and models offers important bits of knowledge into the extraordinary capability of having a significant impact on one's outlook.

Consider the narrative of Song Dweck, an eminent clinician whose work on outlook significantly affects the fields of schooling and brain science. Dweck's examination recognizes two attitudes: the proper outlook and the development mentality. In a decent mentality, people accept that their capacities and knowledge are static qualities. On the other hand, those with a development outlook consider difficulties to be valuable chances to learn and develop.

Dweck's own excursion into the domain of outlook change started with an interest for understanding the reason why a few people bounced back from disappointments while others surrendered to them. Through her examination, she found that people with a development outlook were bound to endure despite difficulties, seeing them not as signs of their intrinsic capacities but rather as venturing stones on the way to progress.

This change in outlook is exemplified in the encounters of understudies who, when shown about the pliability of their knowledge, exhibited expanded inspiration, strength, and an eagerness to embrace difficulties. Dweck's work features the extraordinary force of taking on a development mentality, demonstrating the way that what we see our capacities can significantly mean for our way to deal with learning, our strength notwithstanding misfortunes, and our general direction throughout everyday life.

The excursion of Scratch Vujicic fills in as one more convincing illustration of outlook change. Brought into the world without appendages, Vujicic confronted various physical and inner difficulties since the beginning. However, as opposed to surrendering to surrender, he embraced a mentality portrayed by flexibility, versatility, and a steadfast faith in his own value. Vujicic's story outlines how a change in mentality can empower people to rise above apparently unconquerable hindrances.

Through his persuasive talking, composing, and promotion work, Vujicic motivates others to develop an outlook of appreciation, flexibility, and boundless chance. His life fills in as a demonstration of the possibility that one's mentality can shape individual results as well as effect the existences of everyone around them. Vujicic's extraordinary excursion represents the significant impact of mentality on private prosperity and the capacity to have a constructive outcome on the world.

In the domain of business and business venture, the narrative of Sara Blakely, the organizer behind Spanx, gives an enrapturing contextual investigation in outlook change. Blakely, a previous house to house fax machine sales rep, confronted various dismissals and mishaps on her way to business. Nonetheless, her outlook was portrayed by a steady faith in her own true capacity and a refusal to be deflected by disappointments.

Blakely's extraordinary attitude is clear in her way to deal with difficulties. At the point when she coming up short on fundamental information about the clothing business, she embraced a development mentality, seeing her absence of mastery as a potential chance to advance instead of an obstruction to progress. This point of view enabled her to make Spanx, a billion-dollar shapewear organization that upset the business.

The direction of Sara Blakely's life embodies the effect of a mentality zeroed in on development, flexibility, and a readiness to gain from disappointments. Her story resounds as a demonstration of the possibility that an enterprising outlook, described by flexibility and an eagerness to face challenges, can prompt groundbreaking achievement even notwithstanding starting mishaps.

The field of sports brain science offers various instances of competitors who have bridled the force of outlook change to accomplish maximized operation. Michael Jordan, broadly viewed as one of the best ball players ever, gives an enlightening contextual investigation. Jordan's outlook was set apart by an unwavering quest for greatness, a serious drive, and a capacity to see mishaps as any open doors for development.

Jordan's axiom, "I've flopped again and again in my life. Furthermore, that is the reason I've been effective," epitomizes his mentality of versatility and development.

As opposed to being crippled by disappointments, Jordan involved them as venturing stones to refine his abilities and raise his game. His attitude impelled him to individual accomplishment as well as added to the Chicago Bulls' predominance in the NBA during the 1990s.

The extraordinary force of outlook is additionally exemplified in the tale of Venus and Serena Williams, tennis legends who have reclassified the game. Brought up in Compton, California, the Williams sisters confronted difficulty and doubt because of their experience. Be that as it may, their dad, Richard Williams, imparted in them an outlook of unfaltering self-conviction and strength.

Richard Williams imagined his little girls becoming tennis advocate well before they entered the expert circuit. Through thorough preparation and an emphasis on mental strength, he developed an outlook inside them that rose above the constraints forced by their conditions. The Williams sisters proceeded to become predominant powers in tennis, accomplishing various Huge homerun triumphs and reshaping the scene of ladies' games.

The Williams sisters' process represents the groundbreaking capability of a mentality zeroed in on self-conviction, difficult work, and flexibility. Their story challenges regular stories and highlights how mentality can be an impetus for breaking obstructions and making phenomenal progress.

The universe of science and advancement offers its own variety of attitude change stories. Dr. Sanctuary Grandin, an eminent creature researcher and mental imbalance advocate, epitomizes the effect of utilizing a novel outlook to defeat difficulties. Determined to have chemical imbalance at an early age, Grandin confronted troubles in friendly connections and correspondence. Notwithstanding, her outlook was described by a sharp capacity to think outwardly and sympathize with creatures.

Instead of review her mental imbalance as a constraint, Grandin embraced her extraordinary mental style and utilized it to reform the animals business. Her advancements in creature dealing with frameworks, informed by her capacity to think in pictures, worked on creature government assistance as well as changed the manner in which the business moved toward domesticated animals taking care of. Grandin's story features the force of embracing and utilizing one's exceptional attitude to drive advancement and make positive change.

In the domain of innovation and business venture, the narrative of Elon Musk gives a captivating contextual investigation in mentality change. Musk, the President of SpaceX and Tesla, has reliably shown a mentality portrayed by dauntlessness, flexibility, and a readiness to handle apparently unconquerable difficulties. Musk's aggressive objectives, from colonizing Mars to reforming the car business, mirror an outlook that rises above ordinary limits.

Musk's mentality is one of constant development and a refusal to acknowledge the norm. Indeed, even notwithstanding distrust and mishaps, for example, early monetary battles and specialized difficulties in space investigation, Musk kept an outlook zeroed in on persistent learning and improvement. His groundbreaking effect on the aviation and car ventures outlines the capability of a mentality that joins boldness with a pledge to pushing the limits of what is viewed as conceivable.

The account of J.K. Rowling, the creator of the Harry Potter series, offers a convincing illustration of mentality change in the domain of imagination and writing. Rowling confronted various dismissals from distributers prior to making progress with the Harry Potter books.

Her excursion from battling single parent to quite possibly of the best creator in history is a demonstration of the force of steadiness, versatility, and an outlook that will not be characterized by starting mishaps.

Rowling's mentality is obvious as would be natural for her: "It is difficult to live without falling flat at something except if you live so warily that you should not have inhabited all, in which case you have bombed as a matter of course." This viewpoint embodies an outlook that sees disappointment as an innate piece of the inventive flow and a chance for development. Rowling's extraordinary excursion features the significant effect of a mentality zeroed in on versatility, imagination, and a refusal to be deflected by starting disappointments.

In the domain of wellbeing and health, the account of Dr. Dignitary Ornish delineates the groundbreaking capability of an outlook fixated on way of life and preventive medication. Ornish, a spearheading cardiologist, tested customary clinical insight by upholding for way of life changes, including a plant-based diet, work out, stress the board, and social help, for of forestalling and switching coronary illness.

Ornish's outlook moved the worldview in cardiology, stressing the job of way of life in cardiovascular wellbeing. His examinations showed that thorough way of life changes could prompt critical enhancements in cardiovascular wellbeing, testing the common idea that coronary illness was an irreversible condition. Ornish's work exhibits the extraordinary effect of an outlook that difficulties laid out standards, embraces a comprehensive way to deal with wellbeing, and focuses on preventive measures.

These contextual analyses on the whole outline the significant impact of mentality on one's way of living. Whether in the domains of schooling, business, sports, science, writing, or wellbeing, the force of attitude to shape results is evident. What these accounts share is a repeating theme of flexibility, versatility, and a refusal to be characterized or restricted by outer conditions.

The investigation of these contextual analyses prompts reflection on the elements that add to attitude change. Normal subjects arise, for example, the significance of versatility notwithstanding difficulties, an eagerness to embrace difficulties as any open doors for development, and an immovable confidence in one's capacity to shape their own predetermination. These subjects all in all structure the structure blocks of an extraordinary mentality.

The excursion of mentality change is certainly not a straight way; it is set apart by turns, turns, and snapshots of significant self-disclosure. It requires contemplation, a readiness to challenge restricting convictions, and a pledge to consistent learning. The people for these situation studies didn't accomplish change for the time being; fairly, their accounts unfurl as stories of steadiness, versatility, and an undaunted obligation to developing their viewpoints.

As we inspect these contextual investigations, it becomes evident that outlook change is definitely not a one-size-fits-all undertaking. Every individual's process is novel, molded by their encounters, values, and goals. Notwithstanding, ongoing ideas of mentality, like versatility, flexibility, and a development situated point of view, wind through these different stories, outlining the general rules that underlie extraordinary change.

All in all, the investigation of contextual analyses and instances of people who have changed their lives through significantly impacting their mentality offers a significant look into the unlimited capability of the human brain. Whether defeating affliction, reshaping ventures, or reforming individual prosperity, these accounts act as reference points of motivation. They advise us that the ability to change our lives exists in the domain of our viewpoints, mentalities, and convictions — a domain where the potential for development, strength, and positive change exceeds all rational limitations.

2.3 Discuss the impact of positive thinking and visualization on shaping one's reality

The idea of positive reasoning and representation as apparatuses for molding one's existence has acquired unmistakable quality in self improvement writing, brain research, and self-awareness. The major thought is that the considerations we harbor and the pictures we make to us substantially affect our feelings, ways of behaving, and eventually, the results we experience throughout everyday life. This investigation digs into the significant impact of positive reasoning and perception, looking at how these practices shape one's existence and add to self-improvement, flexibility, and prosperity.

At the center of positive reasoning is the comprehension that our considerations impact our feelings and ways of behaving. Mental social brain science, a broadly perceived restorative methodology, stresses the exchange between considerations, sentiments, and activities. Positive reasoning includes developing a hopeful mentality, zeroing in on productive considerations, and rethinking negative or self-restricting convictions. By deliberately picking positive considerations, people mean to make a psychological scene that cultivates prosperity and flexibility.

Research in brain science has offered exact help for the effect of positive reasoning on psychological wellness and by and large life fulfillment. Studies propose that people who participate in sure reasoning will generally encounter lower levels of pressure, uneasiness, and discouragement. The mental rebuilding intrinsic in certain reasoning includes testing and supplanting pessimistic contemplations with additional hopeful and helpful ones, encouraging a psychological climate helpful for profound prosperity.

In addition, the impact of positive reasoning reaches out to actual wellbeing results. The area of psychoneuroimmunology investigates the association between the brain and the invulnerable framework.

Research demonstrates that an inspirational perspective and hopeful reasoning can add to improved safe capability, better cardiovascular wellbeing, and, surprisingly, expanded life span. The brain body association highlights the complex connection between mental perspectives and actual prosperity.

Positive representation, frequently combined with positive reasoning, makes the idea a stride further by integrating mental symbolism into the most common way of molding one's existence. Perception includes making striking mental pictures of wanted results, achievement, or the accomplishment of explicit objectives. By over and again envisioning these situations, people plan to improve inspiration, fabricate fearlessness, and lay the foundation for transforming their yearnings into the real world.

The effect of positive perception on execution and accomplishment is clear in different spaces, including sports, business, and self-awareness. Competitors, for example, regularly utilize perception procedures to practice effective exhibitions intellectually. By clearly envisioning the execution of abilities, the achievement of objectives, and the experience of win, competitors improve their certainty and prime their psyches for ideal execution.

In the business domain, the force of positive perception is exemplified by fruitful business visionaries and pioneers who characteristic their accomplishments to the act of imagining achievement. By making mental pictures of wanted results, these people develop an outlook that lines up with their objectives, cultivating assurance and constancy. The perception interaction fills in as a mental forerunner to moving toward understanding those yearnings.

The science behind sure perception is established in the mind's ability for brain adaptability — the capacity to redesign itself in light of involvement. At the point when people participate in sure representation, they actuate brain networks related with the envisioned exercises. This interaction prepares to see valuable open doors, perceive assets, and move toward difficulties with a mentality helpful for progress.

Neuroscientific concentrates on utilizing mind imaging advancements have given experiences into the brain components basic the effect of positive perception. The initiation of mind districts related with objective coordinated conduct, inspiration, and close to home guideline recommends that perception impacts mental cycles as well as triggers physiological reactions that add to molding one's world.

The brain science of objective setting adjusts intimately with the standards of positive reasoning and representation. The famous analyst Edwin Locke, as a team with Gary Latham, presented the Objective Setting Hypothesis, placing that particular and testing objectives lead to better execution than dubious or simple objectives.

Positive reasoning and representation assume an essential part in the objective setting process by assisting people with characterizing clear goals, keep up with center, and develop the self-viability expected to seek after and accomplish their desires.

Contextual analyses of people who have utilized positive reasoning and representation to conquer misfortune and make wonderful progress give certifiable instances of the effect of these practices. Consider the narrative of Jim Carrey, the acclaimed entertainer and comic, who broadly kept in touch with himself a check for $10 million bucks prior to accomplishing popularity. Carrey participated in sure representation, envisioning himself as a fruitful entertainer and imagining the monetary prize that would follow. In a momentous new development, Carrey made the degree of progress he had imagined, changing out a $10 million dollar check for his part in the film "Stupid and More idiotic."

Likewise, Oprah Winfrey's excursion from a provoking youth to turning into a news big shot is set apart by her use of positive reasoning and perception. Winfrey has spoken straightforwardly about how she utilized representation procedures to imagine her future achievement. Her capacity to intellectually extend herself into the job of a fruitful moderator and media character added to her steadfast assurance and strength in seeking after her yearnings.

The account of Michael Phelps, the most improved Olympian ever, gives another convincing model. Phelps used a mix of positive reasoning and representation as a feature of his preparation routine. Before each race, he would envision the whole race to him, imagining each stroke, turn, and wrap up with most extreme accuracy. This psychological practice added to Phelps' unmatched concentration, certainty, and capacity to execute his race system with accuracy.

In the domain of business, the example of overcoming adversity of Steve Occupations, prime supporter of Macintosh Inc., highlights the effect of positive reasoning and perception on molding one's existence. Occupations, known for his inventive vision and groundbreaking commitments to the tech business, was a defender of the "truth contortion field." This term, begat by Macintosh representatives, portrays Occupations' capacity to imagine and discuss future prospects with such conviction that it impacted the discernments and activities of everyone around him. Occupations' visionary mentality and positive reasoning assumed a critical part in Apple's prosperity and the formation of momentous items.

Positive reasoning and perception likewise track down application in the field of wellbeing and prosperity. A self-influenced consequence, a peculiarity where people experience genuine upgrades in side effects because of the conviction that a treatment is successful, features the psyche's impact on actual wellbeing. A self-influenced consequence is a demonstration of the force of positive reasoning in getting substantial physiological reactions.

Mind-body mediations, for example, directed symbolism and positive insistence rehearses, have been coordinated into comprehensive ways to deal with wellbeing.

These intercessions expect to tackle the psyche's capability to impact physiological capabilities, diminish pressure, and advance generally prosperity. For instance, people going through clinical therapies or confronting constant circumstances frequently utilize positive perception to upgrade their survival techniques and encourage a more inspirational perspective on their wellbeing.

Logical examinations in the area of psychoneuroimmunology give bits of knowledge into the manners in which positive reasoning and perception influence the resistant framework. Research demonstrates that hopeful perspectives and positive feelings are related with upgraded invulnerable capability, lower levels of irritation, and a diminished gamble of ongoing infections. The psyche's impact on invulnerable reactions highlights the complex association between mental prosperity and actual wellbeing.

The idea of "inevitable outcomes" further explains the effect of positive reasoning on forming one's world. Begat by humanist Robert K. Merton, an unavoidable outcome happens when a conviction or assumption impacts conduct such that makes the conviction work out. With regards to positive reasoning, people who hold hopeful assumptions regarding their capacities, achievement, or connections may unintentionally add to the acknowledgment of those assumptions through their ways of behaving and activities.

While the extraordinary capability of positive reasoning and perception is clear, it is critical to recognize that these practices are not a panacea for all difficulties. Positive reasoning isn't tied in with denying the presence of hardships or embracing a Pollyannaish disposition; rather, it includes moving toward difficulties with a helpful outlook and looking for arrangements with confidence. The critical lies in tracking down a harmony between certain reasoning and a sensible examination of circumstances.

Pundits of positive reasoning contend that an excessively hopeful standpoint might lead people to disregard expected dangers or underrate the work expected to accomplish their objectives. They alert against the risks of "poisonous energy," which includes smothering or negating real feelings for keeping a good façade. A nuanced point of view recognizes the significance of embracing a scope of feelings while utilizing good reasoning as an instrument for versatility and development.

The idea of representation as a device for molding one's existence is established in the conviction that the psyche has a noteworthy ability to impact results through the making of mental pictures. Representation, frequently utilized conversely with mental symbolism or mental practice, includes the deliberate age of definite and striking mental pictures of wanted situations, accomplishments, or objectives. This mental cycle isn't only a whimsical fantasy; rather, a purposeful practice connects with the psyche in a manner that adjusts contemplations, feelings, and activities to make ready for the sign of imagined results.

The fundamental standard of representation lies in the association between the psyche and the body, where the psychological practice of a movement actuates brain networks in the cerebrum related with the actual execution of that action. This peculiarity is supported by the cerebrum's noteworthy brain adaptability — the capacity to revamp itself in view of encounters and mental exercises. At the point when people participate in representation, they animate the very brain processes and region of the mind that would be engaged with the genuine exhibition of the envisioned undertaking, making a powerful scaffold among thought and activity.

Various fields, going from sports brain research to self-improvement and execution enhancement, have perceived and outfit the capability of perception procedures. Competitors, for example, regularly utilize perception as a feature of their preparation routine to intellectually practice developments, upgrade center, and improve execution. By intellectually reproducing the ideal execution of an expertise or the fruitful culmination of a contest, competitors set up their brains and bodies for the difficulties they will look on the field or court.

The effect of representation on sports execution isn't simply narrative; it has accumulated observational help from logical examination. Studies have shown that competitors who integrate representation into their preparation routine experience enhancements in coordinated abilities, strong strength, and in general execution. The psychological symbolism of fruitful results adds to the improvement of a sure outlook, decreased nervousness, and an upgraded capacity to explore high-pressure circumstances.

Past the domain of sports, perception tracks down applications in assorted spaces, including business, the scholarly world, and self-improvement. Business visionaries and business pioneers frequently trait their prosperity to the act of imagining their objectives and business targets. By making a psychological diagram of wanted results, these people develop an outlook that lines up with their desires, encouraging assurance, flexibility, and an essential way to deal with beating difficulties.

In scholarly world, understudies and experts the same influence representation strategies to upgrade learning, further develop center, and improve mental execution. Mental practice of introductions, critical thinking situations, or complex ideas can add to expanded certainty, decreased uneasiness, and further developed memory review. The purposeful making of mental pictures that portray effective scholastic undertakings adds to a positive outlook that upholds accomplishment.

The effect of perception on molding one's world is apparent in self-improvement and objective accomplishment. People who consistently participate in perception rehearses frequently report uplifted inspiration, expanded self-viability, and a feeling of arrangement between their viewpoints and activities. Whether imagining profession achievement, monetary overflow, or individual connections, the purposeful production of mental pictures fills in as a strong impetus for changing desires into substantial reality.

One of the vital instruments through which perception shapes one's world is the effect on inspiration and objective coordinated conduct. The psychological pictures made through perception act as convincing motivators that initiate the mind's award framework. As people clearly picture the achievement of their objectives, the cerebrum discharges synapses like dopamine, building up the association between the imagined result and positive feelings. This neurobiological reaction upgrades inspiration as well as fortifies the obligation to doing whatever it may take to transform the envisioned reality into fact.

The mental idea of self-adequacy, presented by Albert Bandura, further explains the job of representation in shaping way of behaving. Self-viability alludes to a singular's faith in their capacity to effectively execute a specific way of behaving or accomplish a particular result. Perception adds to the improvement of self-viability by furnishing people with a psychological guide of progress. As they more than once envision themselves conquering impediments, showing capability, and accomplishing their objectives, their trust in their capacity to make an interpretation of these psychological pictures into certifiable activities and results develops.

In addition, the effect of representation reaches out to the domain of close to home guideline and stress the board. Representation fills in as a device for making a psychological safe-haven — a protected and positive space where people can withdraw to diminish pressure, develop a feeling of quiet, and improve by and large close to home prosperity. By strikingly envisioning tranquil scenes, positive connections, or snapshots of accomplishment, people can bring out unwinding reactions that balance the physiological impacts of pressure.

The helpful utilizations of representation are obvious in fields, for example, psychotherapy and care rehearses. Directed symbolism, a method that includes driving people through a progression of striking mental pictures, is ordinarily used to address different mental difficulties, including uneasiness, fears, and post-horrendous pressure problem. The deliberate formation of positive mental pictures adds to mental rebuilding, permitting people to reconsider and reevaluate pessimistic idea designs.

The investigation of the effect of perception on forming one's existence crosses with the standards of the Pattern of good following good — a powerful idea that proposes that positive or pessimistic contemplations bring relating encounters into an individual's life. While the Pattern of good following good is frequently met with doubt, its center precepts line up with the mental cycles inborn in perception. The accentuation on purposeful concentration, positive hope, and the conviction that contemplations impact results highlights the interconnected connection between mental states and outside real factors.

True instances of people who quality their prosperity to representation flourish. Think about the narrative of Arnold Schwarzenegger, the notable weight lifter, entertainer, and previous legislative head of California. Schwarzenegger has spoken widely about how he utilized perception methods all through his vocation.

Prior to winning various Mr. Olympia titles, Schwarzenegger would distinctively envision himself on the stage, acting like the boss. This psychological practice added to his actual experience as well as encouraged a mentality of relentless certainty and assurance.

Likewise, Oprah Winfrey, news magnate and giver, has shared how representation assumed a critical part in her excursion to progress. Winfrey imagined herself as an effective moderator some time before she became one. She utilized perception not exclusively to picture her future achievement yet in addition to feel the feelings related with accomplishing her objectives. This purposeful representation added to Winfrey's flexibility, self-adequacy, and the possible acknowledgment of her vision.

The encounters of fruitful people who trait their accomplishments to perception highlight the groundbreaking capability of this training. The deliberate production of mental pictures lines up with the standards of objective setting, mental social brain research, and the inborn association between thought designs and conduct results.

Neuroscientific studies give further bits of knowledge into the components through which representation influences the cerebrum. Useful attractive reverberation imaging (fMRI) studies have shown that psychological symbolism initiates mind areas related with the genuine encounter of the envisioned movement. The cross-over in brain enactment among representation and execution recommends that the mind deciphers clear mental pictures as significant encounters, affecting discernments, feelings, and ensuing activities.

Research in the field of engine symbolism, a particular type of perception zeroed in on development, upholds the thought that psychological practice adds to upgrades in coordinated movements. Studies including competitors, artists, and people recuperating from wounds have shown that taking part in mental symbolism of actual developments upgrades engine learning, coordination, and by and large execution. The mind's versatility permits it to adjust and refine brain associations in view of both physical and envisioned encounters.

The effect of representation isn't restricted to individual pursuits; it stretches out to relational elements and the aggregate attitude inside associations and networks. In hierarchical settings, pioneers who capably convey a convincing vision add to a common mental symbolism that adjusts colleagues toward shared objectives. The making of an aggregate mental picture cultivates a feeling of direction, coordinated effort, and a common obligation to accomplishing hierarchical goals.

While the expected advantages of representation are huge, it is fundamental to recognize that its adequacy might shift among people. Factors like individual contrasts in mental styles, character attributes, and the level of commitment with the represen-tation cycle can impact results.

Also, the particularity and lucidity of the psychological pictures, the close to home force related with them, and the consistency of perception rehearses add to their effect on forming one's world.

Pundits might contend that the viability of perception is dependent upon different variables, including the arrangement of mental symbolism with reasonable objectives, the presence of integral activity steps, and the thought of likely difficulties. Only perception is certainly not a substitute for exertion, expertise improvement, or key preparation. Rather, it works synergistically with deliberate activities and a guarantee to the quest for one's objectives.

In instructive settings, the standards of representation line up with creative ways to deal with educating and learning. Instructive clinicians perceive the benefit of integrating representation strategies to upgrade's comprehension understudies might interpret complex ideas, further develop memory maintenance, and cultivate imagination. Imagining verifiable occasions, logical cycles, or numerical arrangements gives understudies a psychological platform that upholds perception and commitment.

The job of perception in the helpful setting stretches out past directed symbolism to mediations like augmented experience openness treatment. Computer generated reality stages empower people to stand up to and explore mimicked situations in a controlled climate, offering an incredible asset for tending to fears, post-horrendous pressure problem, and nervousness issues. The vivid idea of computer generated reality upgrades the effect of mental symbolism in restorative applications.

The convergence of care practices, reflection, and representation highlights the interconnectedness between present-second mindfulness and purposeful mental symbolism. Care rehearses urge people to develop a non-critical consciousness of their viewpoints and encounters. Integrating perception into care reflection permits people to make positive mental pictures that add to unwinding, stress decrease, and a general feeling of prosperity.

In , the effect of perception on molding one's existence is a dynamic and complex peculiarity that crosses mental, close to home, and physiological aspects. The purposeful production of distinctive mental pictures fills in as an impetus for adjusting contemplations, feelings, and ways of behaving toward the acknowledgment of imagined results. From sports fields to meeting rooms, homerooms to treatment meetings, the standards of perception track down applications in different settings, adding to self-improvement, objective achievement, and in general prosperity.

The exact proof supporting the effect of perception on mental cycles, brain actuation, and execution results highlights the unmistakable impact of mental symbolism on molding one's world.

The encounters of people who property their prosperity to representation give genuine instances of the groundbreaking capability of this training. The interconnected connection between considerations, feelings, and activities features the complicated dance between the brain and the outside world.

Useful utilizations of representation, whether in objective setting, scholastic pursuits, or stress the executives, welcome people to investigate the force of their creative mind as a device for individual and aggregate change. As science keeps on unwinding the secrets of the cerebrum and the brain, the investigation of perception opens roads for outfitting this natural mental capacity to make positive change, develop flexibility, and shape a reality that lines up with one's desires and potential.

Chapter 3

The Influence of Beliefs

The impact of convictions on people and social orders is a significant and diverse peculiarity that shapes the manner in which individuals see and communicate with their general surroundings. Convictions, whether they are strict, social, or individual, assume a vital part in molding one's qualities, perspectives, and ways of behaving. This many-sided trap of convictions characterizes a singular's way of life as well as adds to the aggregate personality of networks and whole civilizations.

At the center of the impact of convictions is the human psyche, a complicated and dynamic substance that processes data, builds importance, and structures decisions in view of the system of convictions it has created after some time. According to a mental viewpoint, convictions act as mental designs that assist people with figuring out their encounters and explore the intricacies of life. These mental designs are profoundly implanted in the psyche mind, impacting points of view and molding the focal point through which people see reality.

Social convictions, established in shared customs, customs, and values, assume a crucial part in forming the shared perspective of social orders. These convictions are in many cases passed down from one age to another, making a feeling of congruity and rationality inside a local area. Social convictions act as the establishment for normal practices, directing way of behaving and encouraging a feeling of having a place among people who share a typical social personality.

Strict convictions, one more huge class of convictions, apply a significant impact on people and social orders around the world. The confidence an individual buys into frequently gives an ethical compass, directing moral choices and molding virtues. In addition, strict convictions can impact social union, as networks with shared strict convictions frequently structure very close bonds that rise above individual contrasts.

The effect of convictions on conduct is obvious in different parts of human existence, going from relational connections to cultural designs. In private connections, people with shared convictions might figure out some mutual interest and a feeling of association, while clashing convictions can prompt pressure and disunity. Likewise, cultural designs, like general sets of laws and administration, are many times impacted by the overarching convictions inside a given culture or local area.

The impact of convictions reaches out past the domain of the individual and cultural to include more extensive worldwide elements. Worldwide relations, international struggles, and social trades are profoundly impacted by the assorted convictions held by various countries and networks. The conflict of convictions can prompt misconceptions, clashes, and, now and again, even viciousness as varying perspectives compete for strength on the worldwide stage.

One of the key components that add to the strength of convictions is their close to home reverberation. Convictions are not simple scholarly builds; they are profoundly interlaced with feelings, frequently summoning overwhelming inclinations of conviction, faithfulness, or even devotion. This close to home aspect adds a layer of power to the impact of convictions, profoundly shaping reasonable idea as well as profoundly instilled close to home reactions.

The job of convictions in molding character is a focal part of their impact. People frequently infer an identity from their convictions, whether these convictions are connected with their social foundation, strict affiliations, or individual qualities. Convictions give a structure through which people characterize who they are, giving a feeling of motivation and heading throughout everyday life.

Nonetheless, the impact of convictions isn't generally a positive power. While convictions can act as wellsprings of motivation, inspiration, and local area union, they can likewise become wellsprings of division, bias, and struggle. History is packed with instances of wars, oppression, and segregation energized by different convictions, featuring the clouded side of conviction frameworks when taken to limits.

The pliability of convictions is one more interesting part of their impact. People and social orders are not static substances; they develop and adjust after some time. Convictions, as well, go through changes because of evolving conditions, new data, and developing accepted practices. The interchange among convictions and cultural change is a unique interaction, with convictions both molding and being formed by the developing scene of human experience.

In the contemporary world, the impact of convictions is additionally amplified by the quick spread of data through innovation and broad communications. The computerized age has introduced a period where convictions can be shared, tested, and intensified on a worldwide scale. Online entertainment stages, specifically, have become milestones for the conflict of convictions, molding public talk and impacting political scenes.

The force of convictions to shape political philosophies and developments is obvious in the ascent of libertarian developments, character legislative issues, and the polarization of social orders. Convictions, whether established in patriotism, populism, or other philosophical systems, can stir masses, prepare political help, and reshape the political scene of whole countries. The crossing point of convictions and legislative issues highlights the expansive ramifications of the impact of convictions on cultural designs.

The school system is another basic field where the impact of convictions is conspicuous. Instructive establishments, from elementary schools to colleges, assume a critical part in forming the convictions and perspectives of people. The educational program, showing techniques, and social setting inside instructive foundations all add to the development of convictions among understudies. The impact of convictions in training reaches out past scholastic subjects to envelop values, morals, and accepted practices.

In addition, the impact of convictions isn't bound to the domain of coordinated religion or formal training. Mainstream conviction frameworks, like belief systems and methods of reasoning, additionally apply a huge effect on people and social orders. Political belief systems, for instance, shape the manner in which people see administration, equity, and cultural designs. Essentially, philosophical convictions about the idea of presence, profound quality, and the motivation behind life can profoundly impact one's perspective and guide moral independent direction.

The unique interaction between individual convictions and cultural designs brings up significant issues about the harmony between private independence and aggregate attachment. While convictions furnish people with a feeling of personality and reason, they can likewise be a wellspring of strain when individual convictions wander from cultural standards. Finding some kind of harmony between individual opportunity of conviction and the requirement for social agreement is a continuous test looked by different social orders all over the planet.

The impact of convictions on emotional well-being is another aspect that warrants investigation. The crossing point of convictions with mental prosperity is a mind boggling interchange that can make both positive and adverse consequences. On one hand, convictions can furnish people with a feeling of significance, trust, and flexibility despite difficulty. Then again, unbending or outrageous convictions can add to mental misery, nervousness, and, surprisingly, emotional wellness problems.

The effect of convictions on dynamic cycles is a vital part of their impact. Convictions act as channels through which people decipher data, survey dangers, and decide. Mental predispositions, impacted by basic convictions, can shape dynamic in unobtrusive ways, driving people to see data in a way reliable with their prior convictions. Understanding the interconnection among convictions and direction is fundamental for resolving issues, for example, tendency to look for predetermined feedback and advancing objective, proof based navigation.

In the domain of science and innovation, the impact of convictions can be both a main impetus and a possible snag. Logical convictions, in light of experimental proof and thorough request, structure the groundwork of how we might interpret the regular world. Notwithstanding, the conflict between logical convictions and profoundly dug in strict or social convictions has been a repetitive subject since the beginning of time, prompting banters over issues, for example, development, environmental change, and clinical progressions.

The impact of convictions on moral contemplations is a basic part of their effect on human way of behaving. Moral systems frequently get from strict or philosophical convictions, directing people in figuring out what is ethically correct or wrong. The variety of moral convictions across societies and religions features the emotional idea of profound quality and the test of figuring out something worth agreeing on in a world with shifting conviction frameworks.

An investigation of the impact of convictions would be inadequate disregarding the job of customs and services. Customs, whether strict or social, are emblematic articulations of convictions that support social bonds and communicate social or strict qualities starting with one age then onto the next. These customs frequently assume a focal part in characterizing aggregate personality and cultivating a feeling of coherence inside networks.

The impact of convictions likewise stretches out to the domain of workmanship and imagination. Imaginative articulations, whether as writing, music, visual expressions, or performing expressions, frequently draw motivation from the convictions and values pervasive in a given society. Workmanship has the ability to challenge existing convictions, incite thought, and rouse change, making it a strong mode for investigating the different features of the human experience molded by conviction frameworks.

As we dig into the impact of convictions, it becomes obvious that the elements are not unidirectional. While convictions shape people and social orders, they, thusly, are formed by the more extensive setting of verifiable, social, and social impacts. The corresponding connection among convictions and outside factors makes a unique input circle, where convictions both reflect and add to the continuous development of human civilization.

The idea of conviction frameworks as unique, developing substances challenges the thought of a fixed and perpetual arrangement of convictions. People might go through significant changes in their convictions throughout their lives, impacted by private encounters, openness to new data, and developing viewpoints. Essentially, cultural conviction frameworks can go through changes because of social movements, mechanical headways, and international changes.

The impact of convictions on human conduct raises moral contemplations, especially when convictions add to separation, bigotry, or brutality. Finding some kind of harmony between regarding individual convictions and advancing qualities that maintain basic freedoms and civil rights is a sensitive test looked by policymakers, instructors, and pioneers at different degrees of society. The requirement for discourse, understanding, and compassion becomes essential in exploring the intricacies of conviction frameworks in a different and interconnected world.

All in all, the impact of convictions on people and social orders is a complex and unavoidable power that shapes human involvement with significant ways. From individual personality to cultural designs, from political philosophies to moral contemplations, convictions penetrate each part of human existence. The interchange between individual convictions and aggregate standards, the close to home reverberation of convictions, and their effect on character, navigation, and conduct all add to the complex embroidery of human life molded by conviction frameworks.

As we explore the perplexing territory of conviction frameworks, it is fundamental for encourage receptiveness, resistance, and an eagerness to take part in productive discourse. Perceiving the variety of convictions and understanding the unique idea of conviction frameworks can make ready for a more comprehensive and amicable conjunction in our current reality where convictions keep on assuming a focal part in molding the past, present, and eventual fate of mankind.

3.1 Investigate the role of beliefs in shaping individual and societal narratives

The job of convictions in molding individual and cultural stories is a significant and multifaceted part of human experience. Convictions, whether established in religion, culture, belief system, or individual qualities, contribute essentially to the accounts we tell ourselves and the more extensive stories that characterize our networks and civilizations.

This investigation digs into the complex manners by which convictions impact the development of accounts, from the individual domain of individual personality to the more extensive setting of cultural stories that shape shared awareness.

At the singular level, convictions act as the establishment whereupon individual accounts are constructed. Since early on, people are presented to a heap of impacts that add to the development of their conviction frameworks. Family, culture, schooling, and individual encounters all assume a part in molding the convictions that people hold about themselves, others, and the world. These convictions, thus, become necessary parts of the accounts people develop to get a handle on their lives.

The stories people make about themselves are not static; they develop over the long run in light of evolving conditions, new encounters, and self-improvement. Convictions assume a significant part in this continuous course of story development, impacting the understanding of occasions, the attribution of importance, and the improvement of a cognizant identity. Positive convictions can encourage versatility, fearlessness, and a feeling of direction, while pessimistic convictions might add to self-uncertainty, tension, and a twisted self-discernment.

The transaction among convictions and individual accounts is especially clear in the domain of personality development. Convictions around one's social foundation, nationality, orientation, and other personality markers add to the accounts that people develop about what their identity is. These character stories, affected by both individual convictions and cultural standards, shape the manner in which people see themselves and how they present their personalities to other people.

Moreover, convictions about private capacities, potential, and value can fundamentally affect the directions of individual lives. The account of self-adequacy, impacted by convictions in one's abilities and organization, can drive people to seek after aggressive objectives, conquer hindrances, and continue despite difficulties. Interestingly, convictions of insufficiency or shamefulness might add to self-restricting stories that impede self-awareness and satisfaction.

The crossing point of individual stories and cultural stories is a perplexing territory where convictions assume a significant part in molding shared mindset. Cultural stories envelop the narratives, values, and fantasies that characterize a local area, country, or progress. These stories are not simple deliberations; they impact normal practices, institutional designs, and the common feeling of personality among individuals from a general public.

Strict convictions, for instance, frequently support the moral and moral structures implanted in cultural accounts. The tales and lessons of strict customs add to the ethical texture of networks, affecting regulations, social practices, and cultural assumptions. The effect of strict convictions on cultural stories can be significant, molding the aggregate comprehension of good and bad and giving an ethical compass that directs the way of behaving of people inside the local area.

Social convictions likewise assume a focal part in forming cultural stories. The tales, customs, and values went down through ages add to the social personality of a local area. These social stories characterize a common legacy, give a feeling of coherence, and cultivate an aggregate personality among people with normal social affiliations. Social convictions impact everything from workmanship and writing to social ceremonies and relational connections, adding to the rich woven artwork of human social orders.

Political philosophies, one more classification of convictions, fundamentally affect cultural accounts. The tales told by political philosophies shape the manner in which people see the job of government, the conveyance of force, and the design of society. Whether through stories of a vote based system, communism, traditionalism, or other political structures, convictions about administration and cultural association impact the development of foundations and the molding of public strategies.

In looking at the job of convictions in cultural stories, recognizing the power elements at play is essential. Prevailing convictions inside a general public frequently direct the standard story, impacting how history is depicted, what voices are heard, and which points of view are underestimated. The contestation of accounts, hence, turns into a milestone for contending convictions, with minimized bunches frequently moving the predominant story to state their own accounts and encounters.

Media and correspondence channels likewise add to the dispersal of cultural stories, and convictions assume a focal part in forming the messages passed on to people in general. The accounts told by the media, whether through news, amusement, or promoting, reflect and support winning cultural convictions. Media stories, thus, can impact popular assessment, shape social mentalities, and add to the propagation or change of cultural accounts.

The impact of convictions on cultural accounts isn't just reflected in the tales that are recounted yet in addition in the narratives that are hushed or excluded. The specific outlining of stories, impacted by winning convictions, can add to the deletion of specific encounters, viewpoints, and voices. This exclusionary dynamic features the significance of fundamentally looking at the job of convictions in molding cultural stories and the possible results of unexamined predispositions.

In addition, the job of convictions in authentic accounts couldn't possibly be more significant. How history is deciphered, recalled, and sent to people in the future is profoundly impacted by the common convictions inside a general public. Verifiable accounts frequently mirror the qualities, predispositions, and points of view of the individuals who hold the ability to shape the narratives that are told. The contestation of verifiable stories turns into a method for testing or supporting existing convictions about character, equity, and the direction of a general public.

The convergence of convictions and cultural accounts is especially apparent in snapshots of cultural disturbance or change. During times of progress, existing stories might be tested, and new accounts might arise as an impression of developing convictions and values. Social developments, political insurgencies, and social moves frequently involve a reconsideration of existing stories, with convictions filling in as impetuses for aggregate activity and social change.

Looking at the impact of convictions on individual and cultural stories likewise requires an investigation of the job of language. Language isn't only a device for correspondence; it is a vehicle for communicating and supporting convictions. The words we use, the allegories we utilize, and the accounts we develop through language shape how we might interpret the world and add to the stories that characterize our individual and aggregate personalities.

The force of language in molding accounts is apparent in the manner in which certain terms become pervaded with importance and implications. Convictions, whether intentionally or unwittingly, impact the language we use to depict ourselves, others, and our general surroundings. The outlining of issues, the selection of words, and the accounts built through language all reflect hidden convictions, affecting discernment and forming the narratives that become imbued in cultural cognizance.

With regards to cultural accounts, the job of instruction is principal. Instructive establishments are channels for sending information as well as strong specialists in molding convictions and stories. The educational plan, course readings, and showing strategies utilized in schools add to the development of cultural accounts by impacting the convictions of progressive ages. The stories introduced in instructive settings can either support existing cultural standards or challenge them, assuming a critical part in molding the points of view of future residents.

The computerized age has carried new aspects to the transaction among convictions and accounts. Web-based entertainment stages, online discussions, and advanced narrating have become powerful spaces where stories are built, spread, and challenged. The democratization of data through computerized stages has permitted people and networks to share their accounts and challenge standard stories, adding to a more pluralistic and various scene of stories.

Nonetheless, the computerized period likewise presents difficulties, including the quick spread of falsehood, protected, closed off areas that support existing convictions, and the control of stories for different purposes. The impact of convictions on advanced stories brings up issues about the job of innovation in either propagating or testing cultural accounts and the obligation of people, stages, and policymakers in exploring this complicated territory.

The effect of convictions on cultural stories isn't bound to a specific social, geological, or verifiable setting. The comprehensiveness of this peculiarity is obvious in the manner convictions shape accounts across assorted social orders and civic establishments.

While the particular substance of convictions might shift, the basic instruments of story development, impacted by conviction frameworks, are an ongoing idea that goes through the texture of human experience.

In taking into account the impact of convictions on stories, moral contemplations come to the front. The force of accounts to shape insights, impact conduct, and effect the direction of social orders highlights the moral obligation of the individuals who employ the pen, the amplifier, or the advanced stage. Moral narrating requires a guarantee to precision, reasonableness, and the consideration of different viewpoints, perceiving the likely outcomes of stories that propagate generalizations, segregation, or foul play.

The job of convictions in forming stories likewise meets with the more extensive philosophical investigation into the idea of truth and subjectivity. Postmodern points of view challenge the thought of genuine truth, featuring the emotional and socially developed nature of stories. From this outlook, accounts are not unbiased portrayals of the real world but rather are molded by the convictions, predispositions, and points of view of the people who build them. The affirmation of this subjectivity welcomes a basic assessment of the power elements innate in story development and the potential for elective stories that challenge predominant standards.

As we explore the many-sided landscape of convictions and stories, it becomes clear that these two components are inseparably connected, impacting and forming each other in a persistent criticism circle. Convictions give the primary system whereupon accounts are built, while stories, thusly, support, challenge, or change existing convictions. This unique exchange happens at both the individual and cultural levels, adding to the rich woven artwork of human experience and the continuous advancement of societies and civilizations.

The examination concerning the job of convictions in molding individual and cultural stories highlights the requirement for a nuanced and interdisciplinary methodology. The areas of brain research, human science, human studies, correspondence studies, and reasoning all contribute important experiences to how we might interpret this mind boggling peculiarity. Besides, the acknowledgment of the variety of convictions and stories across societies and social orders requires a worldwide point of view that rises above restricted social or philosophical limits.

All in all, the investigation of the job of convictions in molding individual and cultural stories uncovers a dynamic and multifaceted transaction that characterizes the human experience. From the tales people tell about themselves to the more extensive stories that mold social orders, convictions apply a significant impact on the development of importance, character, and common perspective. Perceiving the force of convictions in account development welcomes us to participate in basic reflection, moral narrating, and a pledge to encouraging stories that add to the prospering of people and the improvement of social orders.

3.2 Explore the psychology of belief systems and how they impact decision-making

The brain science of conviction frameworks is an intriguing and complex field that digs into the mental, profound, and social components of how people structure, hold, and change their convictions. Conviction frameworks act as mental structures that assist with peopling get a handle on the world, giving a focal point through which they decipher data and explore the intricacies of direction. Understanding the brain research of conviction frameworks is essential in unwinding the complex trap of variables that impact human way of behaving and dynamic cycles.

At the center of the brain research of conviction frameworks is the human requirement for mental consistency, as guessed by analyst Leon Festinger in his fundamental work on mental cacophony. Mental discord hypothesis places that people have a natural drive to keep up with inside consistency in their convictions, perspectives, and values. When faced with clashing data or encounters, people experience uneasiness, provoking them to look for goal through changes in their convictions or ways of behaving.

This intrinsic drive for mental consistency adds to the development of conviction frameworks that are impervious to change. Once settled, convictions become piece of a person's mental character, impacting discernments, translations, and dynamic cycles. The close to home interest in existing conviction frameworks can make a mental hindrance to tolerating new data or viewpoints that challenge those convictions.

The job of feeling in conviction development and upkeep is a pivotal part of the brain research of conviction frameworks. Feelings, like trepidation, euphoria, outrage, and disdain, can essentially impact the manner in which people process data and decide. Convictions frequently become interwoven with profound reactions, making a powerful blend that shapes direction. Genuinely charged convictions might lead people to focus on data that lines up with their profound inclinations and reject data that goes against them.

Besides, social and social impacts assume a urgent part in forming conviction frameworks. Social character hypothesis proposes that people determine a healthy self-appreciation and having a place from their enrollment in gatherings, and convictions related with these gatherings become essential to individual personality. Overall vibes, peer impact, and cultural standards add to the support of shared convictions, making an aggregate conviction framework that impacts decision-production at both the individual and cultural levels.

The effect of social and social elements on conviction frameworks is apparent in the peculiarity of social comprehension, where people structure convictions that line up with the qualities and standards of their social or gatherings.

Social insight hypothesis recommends that people are persuaded to shape convictions that imply their reliability to, and ID with, their social networks. This cycle impacts individual navigation as well as adds to the polarization of convictions inside social orders.

Tendency to look for predictable feedback, a legitimate mental predisposition, is one more key component in the brain research of conviction frameworks. This predisposition alludes to the propensity of people to look for, decipher, and recollect data in a way that affirms their prior convictions while overlooking or making light of data that challenges them. Tendency to look for predictable feedback assumes a critical part in dynamic by molding the manner in which people see proof, evaluate dangers, and settle on decisions that line up with their current convictions.

The job of conviction tirelessness further mixtures the difficulties related with changing conviction frameworks. Conviction diligence is the propensity for people to keep up with their convictions even despite disconnected proof or disconfirming data. When a conviction is solidly settled, people might oppose refreshing their convictions because of the uneasiness related with mental disharmony or a craving to keep a steady perspective.

The brain science of conviction frameworks likewise meets with the more extensive field of roused thinking. Propelled thinking alludes to the cycle by which people participate in specific handling of data, assessing proof in a way that lines up with their previous convictions or wanted ends. This persuaded thinking impacts individual direction as well as adds to the polarization of convictions in cultural talk.

The effect of conviction frameworks on direction turns out to be especially articulated in high-stakes circumstances or when people face vulnerability. In these unique situations, people might depend on heuristics — mental easy routes or general guidelines — to pursue choices rapidly and proficiently. Heuristics are impacted by conviction frameworks, and people might float towards choices that line up with their current convictions as opposed to taking part in careful, impartial data handling.

The impact of conviction frameworks on navigation is apparent in different areas, including governmental issues, financial aspects, wellbeing, and relational connections. Political convictions, for instance, can shape the manner in which people assess strategy proposition, decipher political occasions, and pick political applicants. Monetary convictions might impact monetary navigation, speculation techniques, and perspectives towards abundance appropriation. Wellbeing related convictions can influence choices with respect to way of life decisions, clinical medicines, and preventive ways of behaving.

In relational connections, conviction frameworks assume a significant part in molding correspondence, compromise, and collaboration.

Shared convictions can encourage a feeling of association and understanding, while unique convictions might prompt errors and relational struggles. The impact of conviction frameworks on relational elements features the interconnectedness of individual and aggregate dynamic cycles.

The mental instruments that underlie the effect of conviction frameworks on independent direction are additionally explained by double cycle hypotheses of perception. Double cycle hypotheses suggest that human insight includes two unmistakable frameworks: Framework 1, which is quick, programmed, and instinctive, and Framework 2, which is slow, purposeful, and logical. Conviction frameworks frequently work inside the instinctive and programmed cycles of Framework 1, affecting speedy decisions and choices.

The interaction between Framework 1 and Framework 2 cycles adds to the intricacy of conviction driven navigation. While Framework 1 cycles depend on heuristics, close to home reactions, and speedy decisions affected by conviction frameworks, Framework 2 cycles include more conscious and intelligent thinking. Adjusting these double cycles is fundamental for successful dynamic that considers both instinctive convictions and scientific contemplations.

The brain science of conviction frameworks additionally reveals insight into the peculiarity of disposition conduct consistency. Perspectives, which are evaluative decisions or sentiments about items, individuals, or issues, are firmly connected to conviction frameworks. The consistency among mentalities and conduct is affected by the strength of convictions and the degree to which people see their activities as lining up with their convictions. Understanding this relationship is vital for anticipating and affecting conduct in view of conviction frameworks.

Mental neuroscience research has given important bits of knowledge into the brain instruments related with conviction arrangement and navigation. Neuroimaging studies propose that mind districts like the prefrontal cortex, amygdala, and insula are engaged with handling conviction related data and profound reactions. The cooperation between these mind locales adds to the joining of mental and close to home perspectives in conviction driven navigation.

The pliancy of the cerebrum, as exhibited by neuroscientific research, features the potential for changing conviction frameworks and, subsequently, dynamic cycles. Brain adaptability alludes to the mind's capacity to redesign itself because of involvement and learning. Mediations, for example, mental conduct treatment, care practices, and training, have shown the ability to prompt changes in conviction frameworks and adjust dynamic examples.

The brain research of conviction frameworks likewise meets with conduct financial matters, a field that investigates how mental variables impact monetary independent direction. Conduct financial aspects challenges customary monetary models that accept people pursue reasonable choices in light of utility amplification.

All things considered, it recognizes the effect of mental predispositions, heuristics, and close to home elements, including conviction frameworks, on financial decisions.

The investigation of the brain science of conviction frameworks stretches out to the more extensive setting of cultural ramifications. Understanding the elements of conviction driven direction is vital for tending to cultural difficulties like deception, polarization, and the spread of fanatic belief systems. In a time of data overflow, the job of conviction frameworks in molding popular assessment, impacting political talk, and driving aggregate way of behaving is more articulated than any other time in recent memory.

Tending to the difficulties related with conviction driven direction requires a complex methodology that incorporates training, media education, and intercessions to advance decisive reasoning. Encouraging a consciousness of mental predispositions, helping people to perceive and alleviate the impact of conviction frameworks, and advancing liberality are fundamental parts of endeavors to upgrade dynamic in both individual and cultural settings.

All in all, the brain research of conviction frameworks gives an exhaustive structure to understanding how convictions shape decision-production at the individual and cultural levels. The interaction between mental, close to home, and social elements highlights the intricacy of conviction driven choice making.

3.3 Discuss the concept of limiting beliefs and methods to overcome them

The idea of restricting convictions is a mental peculiarity that investigates how people hold convictions that compel their true capacity, impede self-awareness, and breaking point their capacity to accomplish their objectives. These convictions, frequently profoundly instilled and subliminal, go about as willful imperatives on what people accept they can achieve or who they can turn into. Grasping the idea of restricting convictions and investigating compelling techniques to defeat them is vital for self-awareness, strengthening, and opening one's maximum capacity.

Restricting convictions can appear in different everyday issues, including self-esteem, connections, profession, and wellbeing. These convictions are much of the time framed right off the bat throughout everyday life, impacted by encounters, cultural assumptions, and messages got from soul mates. They make a psychological structure that characterizes the limits of what people accept is workable for themselves. Normal restricting convictions incorporate thoughts of insufficiency, feeling of dread toward disappointment, the inability to embrace success, and a decent mentality that opposes change and development.

One noticeable part of restricting convictions is their effect on confidence and fearlessness. Trusting in one's capacities and value is central for chasing after objectives and exploring life's difficulties.

Restricting convictions, be that as it may, subvert this establishment by presenting questions, self-analysis, and an unavoidable feeling of dishonor. Beating restricting convictions includes testing and reshaping these negative self-discernments to encourage a more sure and engaging self-idea.

The underlying foundations of restricting convictions frequently follow back to youth encounters and early molding. Messages got from guardians, instructors, or friends can shape the manner in which people see themselves and their abilities. For example, steady bad criticism or ridiculous assumptions might add to the advancement of restricting convictions that continue into adulthood. Perceiving the starting points of these convictions is a vital stage during the time spent beating them.

Mental social treatment (CBT) gives a significant system to understanding and tending to restricting convictions. CBT sets that contemplations, sentiments, and ways of behaving are interconnected, and by changing pessimistic idea designs, people can change their profound reactions and ways of behaving. Applying CBT standards to restricting convictions includes recognizing and testing silly or pointless considerations, supplanting them with additional valuable convictions, and developing positive ways of behaving lined up with these new convictions.

One more powerful calculate the propagation of restricting convictions is the peculiarity of tendency to look for predetermined feedback. Preference for non threatening information alludes to the propensity to look for, decipher, and recollect data in a way that affirms previous convictions. People with restricting convictions may inadvertently channel their encounters to approve these pessimistic discernments, making a self-building up cycle. Conquering tendency to look for predetermined feedback includes intentionally searching out proof that difficulties restricting convictions and embracing an additional liberal and objective point of view.

Care rehearses offer successful strategies for beating restricting convictions by advancing mindfulness and present-second mindfulness. Care urges people to notice their considerations without judgment and become mindful of the stories they tell themselves. By creating care, people can confine from programmed pessimistic contemplations related with restricting convictions, encouraging a more noteworthy feeling of clearness, acknowledgment, and the capacity to reexamine pointless reasoning examples.

Positive confirmations, when utilized in a calculated way, can act as an integral asset in testing and changing restricting convictions. Certifications are positive articulations intended to check negative self-talk and support additional enabling convictions. Making customized confirmations that challenge explicit restricting convictions and rehashing them routinely can progressively move thought designs and add to the development of a more certain and valuable outlook.

In addition, the job of social help and correspondence in defeating restricting convictions couldn't possibly be more significant. Offering one's battles and convictions to confided in companions, family, or guides can give important outer points of view and everyday reassurance. The most common way of articulating and talking about restricting convictions frequently carries them into the cognizant mindfulness, making it more straightforward to challenge and reconsider them with the contribution of others.

A development outlook, an idea created by clinician Song Dweck, is instrumental in beating restricting convictions connected with learning and self-awareness. A development mentality includes the conviction that capacities and insight can be created through exertion, devotion, and learning. Embracing a development mentality challenges the thought of fixed capacities and urges people to see difficulties as any open doors for development instead of impossible hindrances.

Envisioning achievement is a strategy that saddles the force of the brain to beat restricting convictions. Representation includes making mental pictures of oneself accomplishing wanted objectives and encountering achievement. By over and again picturing positive results, people can reinvent their psyche mind and support additional enabling convictions about their capacities and potential. Perception fills in as a strong supplement to other mental procedures in defeating restricting convictions.

Setting and accomplishing little, gradual objectives is a successful technique for building certainty and testing restricting convictions. Separating bigger goals into reasonable advances makes a feeling of achievement, showing to people that progress is conceivable. Outcome in these more modest undertakings adds to a positive criticism circle, slowly disintegrating restricting convictions and encouraging a more prominent identity viability.

The job of self-sympathy in conquering restricting convictions is fundamental. Self-sympathy includes treating oneself with graciousness, understanding, and acknowledgment, particularly despite misfortunes or disappointments. People with restricting convictions might be inclined to self-analysis, further supporting pessimistic insights. Creating self-empathy includes recognizing flaws, gaining from botches, and developing a really sustaining and strong inward exchange.

Social and cultural impacts additionally add to the development and propagation of restricting convictions, especially those connected with personality, orientation, and cultural assumptions. Beating these convictions requires basic assessment of cultural standards and the dismissal of restricting generalizations. Strengthening developments and mindfulness crusades that challenge prohibitive cultural stories assume a significant part in cultivating a more comprehensive and engaging climate.

Moreover, captivating in constant learning and looking for new encounters can be instrumental in defeating restricting convictions. Openness to different points of view, procuring new abilities, and venturing beyond one's usual range of familiarity add to self-improvement and the development of convictions about what is attainable. Embracing a mentality of nonstop learning supports that potential isn't fixed however can be ceaselessly evolved and extended.

Journaling is an intelligent practice that can help with the distinguishing proof and change of restricting convictions. Expounding on private encounters, considerations, and feelings gives an organized method for investigating the starting points of restricting convictions and challenge them. Journaling permits people to keep tabs on their development, commend accomplishments, and gain bits of knowledge into repeating thought processes that might add to restricting convictions.

Remedial mediations, for example, psychotherapy and advising, offer proficient direction in defeating restricting convictions. Specialists can assist people with investigating the main drivers of their restricting convictions, challenge contorted thought designs, and foster systems for building flexibility and confidence. Different helpful methodologies, including mental social treatment, argumentative conduct treatment, and acknowledgment and responsibility treatment, can be custom-made to address explicit parts of restricting convictions.

Furthermore, the act of reexamining includes intentionally impacting the manner in which people decipher and see circumstances. Reevaluating permits people to move their viewpoint from a pessimistic or restricting perspective to a more sure and enabling one. This mental rebuilding strategy includes addressing and testing mutilated contemplations and supplanting them with additional fair and helpful translations.

Developing a feeling of appreciation is one more way to deal with neutralizing restricting convictions. Appreciation includes recognizing and valuing the positive parts of life, even despite difficulties. Zeroing in on appreciation helps shift consideration away from saw deficiencies or restrictions, encouraging a more hopeful and liberal standpoint.

Eventually, conquering restricting convictions is a dynamic and progressing process that requires mindfulness, deliberate exertion, and a promise to self-improvement. Perceiving and testing restricting convictions is a groundbreaking excursion that engages people to rethink their self-idea, seek after their yearnings with certainty, and lead additional satisfying lives. The techniques examined give a far reaching tool stash to people trying to break liberated from the imperatives of restricting convictions and open their maximum capacity.

Chapter 4

Reality Creation through Intention

Reality creation through expectation is an idea established in the possibility that our considerations and convictions straightforwardly affect our general surroundings. It proposes that by adjusting our goals to our cravings, we can shape and form our world to match our dreams. This idea is frequently connected with different profound and magical lessons, yet it likewise tracks down reverberation in mental and logical points of view.

At its center, reality creation through goal is about the force of the psyche to impact the outside world. This thought has been investigated and talked about in different societies and conviction frameworks since the beginning of time. The old way of thinking of Hermeticism, for instance, underscores the standard of mentalism, declaring that the universe is a psychological build and that the brain assumes an essential part in molding reality.

As of late, the idea has acquired prominence through crafted by creators like Neville Goddard, who stressed the job of creative mind and presumption in making one's world. Goddard's lessons recommend that by distinctively envisioning and feeling the satisfaction of our cravings, we can put forth these psychological pictures for the psyche mind, which then attempts to bring those longings into actual reality.

This approach isn't restricted to a specific strict or otherworldly custom; rather, it rises above such limits and is viewed as a widespread standard. It lines up with the possibility that cognizance is an imaginative power and that our contemplations and goals are strong instruments for molding the world we experience.

One vital part of reality creation through expectation is the comprehension that our convictions go about as channels through which we decipher and connect with the world. Assuming we hold restricting convictions about ourselves or our conditions, those convictions can become inevitable outcomes, obliging our true capacity and impacting the results we experience.

In actuality, taking on enabling convictions and setting positive goals can open up additional opportunities and make a better reality. This change in mentality includes a cognizant work to supplant negative idea designs with positive ones, encouraging a feeling of organization and command over one's life.

The job of expectation truly creation is firmly connected to the idea of the general rule that good energy attracts good. The pattern of good following good places that like draws in like, recommending that the energy we discharge through our viewpoints and feelings draws in comparing encounters into our lives. By adjusting our aims to positive energy, we evidently draw positive results and potential open doors towards us.

Nonetheless, moving toward the idea of reality creation through goal with a fair perspective is fundamental. While the force of positive reasoning and expectation setting is recognized by a lot of people, it's anything but a panacea for all difficulties. Outer variables, cultural designs, and unanticipated conditions likewise assume a part in molding our encounters.

Also, pundits contend that an excessively shortsighted understanding of reality creation through aim can prompt casualty accusing, suggesting that people are exclusively liable for their conditions. Actually, foundational issues and outer elements outside of a singular's reach can altogether affect their chances and results.

In any case, defenders of reality creation underscore the significance of getting a sense of ownership with one's viewpoints and expectations. This includes developing mindfulness and care to perceive and move negative idea designs. Thusly, people can become dynamic members in the co-formation of their existence.

In the domain of brain science, the investigation of the brain's effect on conduct and results has brought about the field of positive brain research. Positive brain research investigates factors that add to a satisfying and significant life, underlining the significance of qualities, ethics, and positive feelings.

Specialists in certain brain research have explored the effect of confidence and positive reasoning on emotional well-being and prosperity. Studies propose that people who keep an uplifting perspective might encounter lower levels of pressure, better actual wellbeing, and expanded flexibility notwithstanding challenges.

A self-influenced consequence is another fascinating peculiarity that meets with the idea of reality creation through expectation. In clinical examination, fake treatments — substances with no restorative impact — are some of the time utilized as controls in clinical preliminaries. Shockingly, patients given fake treatments frequently report upgrades in their side effects, featuring the impact of conviction and assumption on actual prosperity.

The psyche body association is a focal subject in understanding what goal can mean for actual wellbeing. Rehearses like care contemplation and directed symbolism have been displayed to decidedly affect different ailments, supporting that the brain can impact the body's mending processes.

The investigation of reality creation through goal likewise dives into the idea of cognizance itself. According to a supernatural viewpoint, cognizance is viewed as the basic texture of the real world. In this view, the outside world is an impression of our inward cognizance, and by changing our awareness, we can modify the truth we experience.

Quantum material science, with its investigation of the way of behaving of particles at the subatomic level, has given grain to conversations on the interchange among cognizance and reality. A few understandings of quantum mechanics propose that the demonstration of perception impacts the result of tests, bringing up issues about the job of cognizance in forming the actual world.

Nonetheless, it's critical to take note of that the connection between quantum physical science and cognizance is a subject of progressing banter among researchers and scholars. While some propose an association, others contend that quantum peculiarities don't be guaranteed to suggest an immediate connection to cognizance or the capacity to shape reality intentionally.

The idea of reality creation through aim is in many cases outlined concerning appearance — the most common way of bringing wanted results into reality through centered thought and expectation. Appearance rehearses range from representation and assertions to customs and services, each expecting to bridle the force of expectation to emerge explicit objectives.

Perception is a regularly involved strategy in sign, including the making of itemized mental pictures of wanted results. Supporters of this training contend that by more than once envisioning an objective as currently accomplished, people send a strong message to their psyche minds, adjusting their contemplations and convictions to the ideal reality.

Insistences, then again, are positive explanations rehashed fully intent on building up a specific conviction or objective. The thought is that by reliably asserting positive convictions, people can reconstruct their psyche minds, steadily moving their thinking designs and drawing in comparing encounters.

Customs and services related with appearance frequently integrate representative activities and motions. These customs can go from straightforward day to day practices to additional intricate services, each intended to intensify the energy and aim behind the indication cycle.

Essential to the viability of these practices is the close to home charge behind the aim. It's not just about precisely rehashing words or envisioning pictures; it's tied in with implanting these activities with authentic inclination and conviction. The close to home perspective is accepted to be a critical consider motioning toward the psyche mind the significance and realness of the ideal result.

Notwithstanding the developing fame of sign practices, doubters contend that the adequacy of such strategies is emotional and fluctuates from one individual to another. A self-influenced consequence, mental inclinations, and the job of specific consideration are refered to as likely clarifications for the apparent progress of sign practices.

While the discussion proceeds, numerous people validate the extraordinary force of aim and sign in their lives. Individual accounts overflow with accounts of individuals conquering difficulties, accomplishing objectives, and showing positive changes subsequent to taking on purposeful practices.

One basic part of reality creation through aim is the idea of separation. Separation includes relinquishing the urgent requirement for a particular result and confiding in the unfurling of the universe. Perplexingly, it's contended that the less joined one is to a specific outcome, the more probable it is to show.

Separation is established in the comprehension that exorbitant connection and obstruction can make vigorous blocks, upsetting the normal progression of appearance. By delivering connection to the result, people permit space for the universe to do something amazing and achieve the most adjusted and helpful outcomes.

This standard lines up with the lessons of different profound customs, where give up and trust are underlined as fundamental parts of the sign interaction. Whether outlined as giving up to a higher power, the universe, or the innate insight of life, the thought is to surrender the deception of control and open oneself to the more noteworthy insight at play.

With regards to reality creation through expectation, the idea of time likewise assumes a critical part. A few lessons recommend that time is definitely not an outright, direct develop yet rather an adaptable and pliant aspect. According to this viewpoint, the past, present, and future exist all the while, and by modifying one's impression of time, people can impact the unfurling of occasions.

The force of now, as promoted by Eckhart Tolle, is a part of this fleeting viewpoint. Tolle accentuates the significance of being completely present in the ongoing second, contending that genuine change and appearance happen in the at this point. Harping on disappointments or restlessly expecting the future, as indicated by Tolle, can hinder the sign interaction.

As opposed to the straight perspective on time, a few profound and mystical lessons propose the presence of equal real factors or substitute aspects. The thought is that each decision we make makes an expanding way, prompting the development of various equal timetables. By moving our cognizance and expectation, defenders of this view recommend that we can explore between these real factors and pick the encounters we need to show.

The investigation of equal real factors achieves forward questions the idea of decision and choice. In the event that each chance exists all the while, does this mean our lives are foreordained, or do we have the office to effectively shape our encounters? The convergence of destiny, predetermination, and unrestrained choice adds intricacy to the comprehension of reality creation through goal.

A urgent component during the time spent reality creation is mindfulness. Developing mindfulness includes becoming aware of one's viewpoints, convictions, and feelings. It requires a legitimate assessment of imbued examples and molding that might be impacting one's view of the real world.

Care rehearses, like contemplation and self-reflection, are significant instruments for creating mindfulness. These practices empower people to notice their contemplations without judgment, cultivating a more profound comprehension of the psychological propensities that might be adding to their ongoing reality.

The idea of the "shadow self," as investigated top to bottom via Carl Jung, is applicable to the excursion of mindfulness. The shadow self addresses the oblivious parts of the mind — the covered up and frequently subdued components that impact conduct and insight.

Coordinating the shadow includes recognizing and embracing these viewpoints, prompting more prominent completeness and mindfulness.

The excursion of mindfulness likewise includes perceiving and delivering restricting convictions. Restricting convictions are profoundly instilled feelings that oblige one's true capacity and conceivable outcomes. They frequently come from youth encounters, cultural molding, or negative self-insights.

Recognizing and testing restricting convictions is a urgent move toward the course of reality creation. By supplanting these restricting considerations with engaging ones, people can move their mentality and open themselves to new open doors and encounters.

The force of language in molding the truth is one more aspect of reality creation through expectation. The words we use, both inside and remotely, convey critical load in impacting our encounters. Positive and enabling language can build up a valuable mentality, while negative or self-restricting language might propagate a pattern of cynicism.

Notwithstanding mindfulness, the development of a positive and thankful outlook is viewed as fundamental truly creation. Appreciation is seen as a strong power that adjusts people to positive energy and draws in a greater amount of what they appreciate into their lives. Practices, for example, keeping an appreciation diary or offering thanks everyday are normal suggestions for encouraging this mentality.

The idea of reality creation through expectation isn't bound to individual encounters; it reaches out to the shared mindset and cultural designs. Defenders of this thought contend that as additional people adjust their goals to positive and amicable results, the shared perspective goes through an extraordinary shift.

This aggregate shift is viewed as an impetus for more extensive cultural changes, going from shifts in social qualities to headways in innovation and science. The interconnectedness of individual and aggregate aim features the potential for an expanding influence, where positive changes at the singular level add to a more amicable and developed worldwide cognizance.

Be that as it may, the possibility of aggregate expectation and its effect on cultural designs is met with suspicion by the people who accentuate the job of foundational issues and institutional designs in forming aggregate encounters. Pundits contend that ascribing social change exclusively to individual or aggregate expectation misrepresents the perplexing interchange of verifiable, financial, and political variables.

In spite of the discussions and shifting points of view, the investigation of reality creation through aim keeps on enrapturing the personalities of people trying to grasp the idea of awareness and its job in molding reality. The combination of profound, magical, mental, and logical bits of knowledge gives a multi-faceted system to looking at the connection among psyche and matter.

As people explore their own excursions of reality creation, it's crucial for approach the idea with insight and a nuanced understanding. Perceiving the interconnectedness of individual expectation with outside factors takes into consideration a more adjusted and reasonable viewpoint on the co-making of the real world.

Taking everything into account, reality creation through goal welcomes people to investigate the significant association among psyche and reality. Whether saw from the perspective of old insight, present day brain science, or supernatural hypothesis, the idea highlights the groundbreaking capability of cognizant idea and expectation.

By adjusting one's contemplations, convictions, and feelings with good and enabling expectations, people might open additional opportunities and shape a reality that lines up with their most profound longings. The excursion of reality creation includes mindfulness, the arrival of restricting convictions, and the development of a positive outlook. It stretches out past the person to envelop the shared mindset, recommending the potential for a far reaching influence of positive change in the more extensive cultural scene.

While the idea of reality creation through aim isn't without its doubters and pundits, the encounters of the people who validate its groundbreaking power won't be quickly excused. As how we might interpret cognizance, quantum physical science, and the idea of reality keeps on developing, the investigation of goal as an imaginative power welcomes continuous request and examination.

At last, reality creation through goal welcomes people to step into the job of cognizant co-makers in the unfurling embroidery of presence. It supports a reexamination of the stories we tell ourselves, the convictions we hold, and the goals we set, perceiving the significant impact these components have on the truth we all in all occupy.

4.1 Examine the connection between intention and manifestation

The association among aim and sign lies at the core of different profound, mystical, and mental methods of reasoning. An idea proposes our considerations, convictions, and cognizant cravings have the ability to shape the truth we experience. To comprehend this association, it's critical to dive into the mind boggling elements among expectation and the method involved with bringing wanted results into reality — appearance.

At its center, aim alludes to a cognizant choice or reason behind an activity. It is the psychological and profound energy coordinated toward a particular objective or result. At the point when people set goals, they are basically adjusting their concentration, will, and wants with a specific vision or goal. This deliberate center is accepted to start a progression of fiery cycles that impact the outside world.

Indication, then again, is the acknowledgment or emergence of something through these purposeful cycles. The substantial result or experience lines up with the first aim. Indication is much of the time portrayed as the extension between the psychological and actual domains, where considerations and wants progress into concrete, perceptible reality.

The excursion from aim to sign includes a few key components. Perception is a noticeable strategy utilized in this cycle. By making distinctive mental pictures of the ideal result, people mean to put forth these pictures for their psyche minds. This, thusly, is accepted to actuate the subliminal to pursue adjusting the outside reality to the inner vision.

Certifications supplement the representation cycle by integrating positive proclamations that build up the planned result. The reiteration of certifications serves to reconstruct the psyche mind, progressively moving instilled thought examples and convictions. The goal, when imbued with certified feeling and conviction, is remembered to convey an intense vivacious charge, impacting the sign cycle.

The pattern of good following good is a fundamental standard in grasping the association among expectation and sign. This regulation recommends that like draws in like — that the energy one puts out into the universe, whether positive or negative, draws comparing encounters and conditions. In this structure, setting positive aims adjusts one's energy to positive results, improving the probability of appearance.

Notwithstanding, it means a lot to move toward the idea of the pattern of good following good with a nuanced viewpoint. Pundits contend that misrepresented translations can prompt a pompous mentality towards outside factors, crediting all results exclusively to individual considerations and goals. While individual organization is stressed, recognizing the impact of outer conditions and fundamental variables is vital for a thorough comprehension.

A self-influenced consequence in clinical settings gives a lined up with the association among aim and sign. A self-influenced consequence happens when people experience genuine upgrades in their circumstances subsequent to getting a treatment with no remedial worth. This peculiarity highlights the job of conviction and assumption in affecting physical and mental prosperity.

The brain body association is one more part of this unpredictable relationship. Practices, for example, care contemplation and directed symbolism show the way that cognizant goal and mental center can affect physiological cycles. Logical investigations have investigated the beneficial outcomes of these practices on pressure decrease, torment the executives, and in general prosperity, proposing an immediate connection among aim and actual results.

The investigation of expectation and sign likewise digs into the domain of quantum physical science, where the way of behaving of particles at the subatomic level difficulties customary ideas of circumstances and logical results. A few understandings of quantum mechanics suggest that the demonstration of perception itself impacts the result of tests, bringing up captivating issues about the job of cognizance in molding reality.

While the association between quantum peculiarities and cognizance stays a subject of discussion, the equals between the two have prompted hypothesis about the flexibility of reality through purposeful concentration. The possibility that cognizance assumes a basic part in the idea of reality lines up with otherworldly and powerful points of view that view awareness as the imaginative power behind presence.

Equal real factors or substitute aspects address one more fascinating feature of the association among expectation and sign. A few speculations recommend that each decision we make prompts the formation of numerous equal courses of events, each addressing an alternate result. By moving one's cognizance and aim, advocates of this view suggest that people can explore between these equal real factors and pick the encounters they need to show.

Separation arises as a basic component during the time spent indication. Separation includes relinquishing the urgent requirement for a particular result and confiding in the normal unfurling of occasions. Oddly, it is contended that the less connected one is to a specific outcome, the more probable it is to show. Separation is established in the comprehension that unnecessary connection and obstruction can make fiery blocks, preventing the regular progression of appearance.

Time, with regards to aim and sign, expects a unique job. A few points of view suggest that time is definitely not a flat out, direct develop yet rather an adaptable and pliable aspect. The idea of the "force of now," advocated by Eckhart Tolle, underscores the significance of being completely present in the ongoing second. As per Tolle, genuine change and sign happen in the present, and harping on disappointments or restlessly expecting the future can hinder the appearance cycle.

The force of language in molding reality likewise assumes a critical part in the association among goal and sign. The words we use, both inside and remotely, convey critical load in affecting our encounters. Positive and enabling language can support a helpful mentality, while negative or self-restricting language might sustain a pattern of cynicism.

The excursion from expectation to indication requires mindfulness — a profound comprehension of one's viewpoints, convictions, and feelings. Care rehearses, like contemplation and self-reflection, act as significant instruments for creating mindfulness. These practices empower people to notice their contemplations without judgment, cultivating a more profound comprehension of the psychological propensities that might be adding to their ongoing reality.

The idea of the "shadow self," as investigated top to bottom via Carl Jung, is applicable to the excursion of mindfulness with regards to sign. The shadow self addresses the oblivious parts of the mind — the covered up and frequently stifled components that impact conduct and discernment. Coordinating the shadow includes recognizing and embracing these perspectives, prompting more prominent completeness and mindfulness.

Testing and delivering restricting convictions is a urgent move toward the course of reality creation. Restricting convictions are profoundly instilled feelings that compel one's true capacity and conceivable outcomes. They frequently come from youth encounters, cultural molding, or negative self-discernments. Recognizing and supplanting these restricting contemplations with engaging ones permits people to move their outlook and open themselves to new open doors and encounters.

The force of goal stretches out past individual encounters to incorporate the shared perspective and cultural designs. Defenders of this thought contend that as additional people adjust their expectations to positive and amicable results, the shared perspective goes through an extraordinary shift. This aggregate shift is viewed as an impetus for more extensive cultural changes, going from shifts in social qualities to headways in innovation and science.

Nonetheless, it's fundamental to recognize the intricacies of ascribing social change exclusively to individual or aggregate goal. Pundits contend that fundamental issues and institutional designs assume a critical part in molding aggregate encounters. While deliberate endeavors can add to positive change, tending to foundational imbalances and supporting for primary changes is similarly critical for enduring cultural change.

All in all, the association among expectation and sign reveals a powerful exchange between the brain and the outside world. Whether saw from the perspective of antiquated intelligence, present day brain science, or mystical hypothesis, this association highlights the extraordinary capability of cognizant idea and goal.

By adjusting one's contemplations, convictions, and feelings with good and enabling goals, people might open additional opportunities and shape a reality that reverberates with their most profound cravings.

The excursion from expectation to indication includes mindfulness, the arrival of restricting convictions, and the development of a positive mentality. It reaches out past the person to envelop the shared perspective, proposing the potential for a gradually expanding influence of positive change in the more extensive cultural scene.

While doubters and pundits offer legitimate points of view, the encounters of the individuals who confirm the groundbreaking force of goal won't be quickly excused. As how we might interpret cognizance, quantum material science, and the idea of reality keeps on developing, the investigation of aim as an inventive power welcomes progressing request and examination.

At last, the association among aim and appearance welcomes people to partake in the co-formation of their existence effectively. It empowers a reconsideration of the narrative.

4.2 Discuss the law of attraction and its role in shaping personal experiences

The pattern of good following good, a broadly examined and discussed idea, proposes that the energy people produce through their viewpoints and feelings draws in relating encounters into their lives. Established in the possibility that like draws in like, the pattern of good following good places that the vibrations people produce into the universe are reflected in the occasions and conditions they experience. Understanding the pattern of energy attracting similar energy and its implied job in forming individual encounters includes investigating its standards, applications, and the nuanced viewpoints that encompass it.

At its center, the pattern of good following good states that people have the ability to show their cravings by adjusting their contemplations and sentiments to the results they look for. This arrangement is accepted to set into movement a progression of occasions and conditions that lead to the satisfaction of those longings. The pattern of good following good is frequently connected with the force of positive reasoning, underlining the significance of keeping a positive mentality to draw in certain results.

Representation is a critical practice inside the structure of the pattern of good following good. It includes making point by point mental pictures of the ideal results, distinctively envisioning the satisfaction of one's objectives. Defenders of perception contend that this cycle sends a strong message to the psyche mind, adjusting it to the planned reality. By more than once picturing an ideal result as though it has proactively happened, people expect to program their psyche brains to pursue bringing that result into actual reality.

Confirmations supplement perception in the act of the general rule that good energy attracts good. Confirmations are positive explanations or statements that people rehash to support a specific conviction or objective.

The redundancy of confirmations is thought to reinvent the psyche mind, step by step supplanting restricting convictions with enabling ones. This change in outlook is viewed as essential for the effective use of the general rule that good energy attracts good.

Pundits, be that as it may, raise worries about the distortion of the pattern of good following good and its capability to advance a "fault the person in question" mindset. They contend that ascribing all life conditions exclusively to one's viewpoints and feelings misrepresents the complicated transaction of outer variables, foundational issues, and underlying imbalances that add to individual encounters. While individual mentality and goal are recognized, pundits stress the significance of resolving more extensive cultural issues for significant change.

The job of feelings in the pattern of good following good is a key perspective that adds profundity to its comprehension. Feelings are viewed as strong marks of one's vibrational recurrence, impacting the energy people emanate into the universe. Positive feelings, like bliss, appreciation, and love, are accepted to draw in good encounters, while pessimistic feelings, like trepidation, uncertainty, and disdain, may draw in ominous results. Overseeing and moving one's personal state becomes fundamental in the act of the general rule that good energy attracts good.

Separation arises as a pivotal standard inside the pattern of good following good. Separation includes relinquishing the urgent requirement for a particular result and confiding in the normal unfurling of occasions. Oddly, it is contended that the less connected one is to a specific outcome, the more probable it is to show. Separation is established in the comprehension that over the top connection and obstruction can make lively blocks, frustrating the regular progression of sign.

Time is one more aspect to think about with regards to the pattern of energy attracting similar energy. A few points of view recommend that time is definitely not an outright, straight develop but instead an adaptable and flexible aspect. The idea of the "force of now," promoted by Eckhart Tolle, lines up with the general rule that good energy attracts good, underlining the significance of being completely present in the ongoing second. Harping on disappointments or tensely expecting what's in store is accepted to hinder the appearance cycle.

The force of language in molding individual encounters is a critical part of the pattern of good following good. The words people use, both inside and remotely, convey significant load in affecting their encounters. Positive and enabling language can support a productive outlook, while negative or self-restricting language might propagate a pattern of cynicism. Becoming aware of one's language turns into a critical part in the deliberate act of the pattern of good following good.

Experimentally, the general rule that good energy attracts good has been met with suspicion, as the proof supporting its standards is to a great extent narrative. Pundits contend that the absence of exact proof difficulties the legitimacy of the pattern of good following good as an all inclusive guideline overseeing individual encounters. While concentrates on in certain brain science feature the advantages of a positive mentality, the immediate connection among's contemplations and outer occasions stays a hostile point.

Lined up with the general rule that good energy attracts good, a self-influenced consequence in clinical settings gives a fascinating examination. A self-influenced consequence happens when people experience genuine upgrades in their circumstances subsequent to getting a treatment with no restorative worth. This peculiarity highlights the job of conviction and assumption in impacting physical and mental prosperity, repeating that cognizance assumes a critical part in molding individual encounters.

The pattern of good following good crosses with different otherworldly and mystical methods of reasoning that view cognizance as a central inventive power. In these systems, the outer world is viewed as an impression of one's inward cognizance, and by changing one's awareness, people can modify the truth they experience. This viewpoint lines up with antiquated shrewdness customs that underline the force of the psyche in forming individual fates.

Be that as it may, the pattern of good following good isn't without its faultfinders and doubters. Some contend that its standards distort the intricacies of life and may prompt a cavalier demeanor toward outer difficulties and foundational issues. Pundits feature the risk of casualty accusing, affirming that crediting all life conditions exclusively to one's viewpoints and feelings ignores the effect of outer variables past individual control.

From a mental point of view, the investigation of mental inclinations offers bits of knowledge into the manners in which people see and decipher their encounters. Tendency to look for predictable feedback, for instance, alludes to the propensity to lean toward data that affirms previous convictions. With regards to the pattern of energy attracting similar energy, people may specifically zero in on sure results that line up with their convictions while ignoring disconnected proof.

While the pattern of energy attracting similar energy is frequently connected with individual achievement and material indications, its standards reach out to different parts of life, including connections and prosperity. The possibility that one's considerations and feelings add to the nature of connections and generally life fulfillment is a focal precept of the pattern of good following good. By deliberately adjusting aims to positive results, people might look to improve their material conditions as well as their general feeling of satisfaction.

The general rule that good energy attracts good is likewise interlaced with the idea of overflow mentality versus world view limited by fear. An overflow mentality is portrayed by a confidence in the endless conceivable outcomes and assets accessible, cultivating an uplifting perspective and receptiveness to potential open doors. Going against the norm, a viewpoint that everything is limited is set apart by an anxiety toward need and impediment, possibly prompting negative idea designs and a cut off point of view. The pattern of good following good urges people to develop an overflow outlook to draw in certain encounters.

In spite of the continuous discussions and changing viewpoints, numerous people verify the groundbreaking force of the pattern of good following good in their lives. Individual accounts swarm with accounts of individuals conquering difficulties, accomplishing objectives, and showing positive changes subsequent to taking on deliberate practices lined up with the pattern of energy attracting similar energy. While episodic proof doesn't comprise logical verification, these tributes add to the continuous exchange encompassing the pattern of energy attracting similar energy.

All in all, the pattern of good following good consumes a special space in the crossing point of otherworldliness, mysticism, brain science, and self-improvement. Its standards, revolved around the possibility that considerations and feelings shape individual encounters, welcome people to take part in the production of their world deliberately. The accentuation on certain reasoning, representation, and profound administration highlights the conviction that deliberate arrangement with wanted results can prompt their indication.

Notwithstanding, a decent point of view recognizes the intricacies of life, the impact of outside factors, and the requirement for resolving fundamental issues. The pattern of good following good, while offering experiences into the force of mentality and aim, ought not be seen as a one-size-fits-all arrangement. All things considered, it fills in as a device that people can decide to integrate into their lives, perceiving the concurrence of individual organization and outer impacts in forming the embroidery of individual encounters.

4.3 Provide practical exercises for setting and aligning intentions

Setting and adjusting goals is a strong practice that permits people to zero in their energy and consideration on wanted results. The cycle includes explaining one's objectives, cultivating a positive mentality, and making deliberate moves to bring those yearnings into the real world. To make aim setting more useful and viable, different activities and procedures can be integrated into day to day existence. These activities mean to improve mindfulness, the capacity to understand people on a profound level, and the capacity to show positive change. The following are a few commonsense activities for setting and adjusting goals:

1. **Careful Breathing and Focusing:**
   Start by tracking down a calm and agreeable space. Sit or rests and take a couple of full breaths to focus yourself. Center around your breath, permitting it to turn out to be slow and cadenced.
   As you breathe in, envision taking in clearness and smoothness. As you breathe out, discharge any pressure or questions. This exercise makes a focused and grounded state, giving a strong groundwork to setting clear expectations.

2. **Representation and Vision Board Creation:**
   Representation is a useful asset for adjusting goals to wanted results. Begin by envisioning your objectives as though they have previously been accomplished. Picture the subtleties and feelings related with the achievement. To improve this interaction, make a dream board by gathering pictures, statements, and images that address your yearnings. Place the vision board in a noticeable area as a day to day sign of your goals.

3. **Positive Attestations:**
   Make positive attestations that line up with your expectations. These certifications ought to be current state, as though your objectives have previously been understood. For instance, on the off chance that you will likely develop a feeling of overflow, your certification could be, "I'm thankful for the overflow that streams into each part of my life." Rehash these confirmations consistently,

either quietly or without holding back, to build up good convictions and shift your mentality.

4. **Journaling for Clearness:**

   Keep a diary devoted to your expectations. Record your objectives, yearnings, and the means you intend to take to accomplish them. Consider the feelings related with your goals and any possible difficulties. Normal journaling gives lucidity, distinguishes designs, and takes into consideration continuous refinement of your aims as you progress on your excursion.

5. **Putting forth Brilliant Objectives:**

   Use the Shrewd models (Explicit, Quantifiable, Attainable, Pertinent, Time-Bound) while characterizing your goals. Obviously lucid what you need to accomplish, guarantee it is quantifiable, set reasonable assumptions, adjust it to your more extensive objectives, and lay out a time period for consummation. Brilliant objectives give an organized structure that upgrades the viability of expectation setting.

6. **Appreciation Practice:**

   Develop an appreciation practice to adjust your goals to positive energy. Every day, offer thanks for parts of your life, both of all shapes and sizes. This training shifts your concentration toward the positive, encouraging an outlook of overflow. Appreciation adjusts your energy to the decency in your life, establishing a climate helpful for showing your goals.

7. **Careful Development and Yoga:**

   Participate in careful development or yoga to associate your body and psyche. These practices advance actual prosperity as well as develop care and presence. As you travel through the stances or activities, center your psyche around your aims. Utilize this chance to envision your objectives and feel the sensations related with accomplishing them.

8. **Directed Reflection for Goal Setting:**

   Investigate directed reflections explicitly intended for goal setting. Numerous reflection applications and online stages offer directed meetings that walk you through the method involved with explaining your expectations and picturing their acknowledgment. These meetings frequently consolidate unwinding procedures to make a responsive mental state for goal setting.

9. **Positive Composition:**

   Compose assertions as sure, explanatory articulations about your goals. For instance, rather than saying, "I need to be more sure," express, "I'm what is happening." Rehash these confirmed assertions consistently, permitting them to become imbued in your psyche mind.

10. **Responsibility Accomplice or Gathering:**

    Share your goals with a confided in companion, relative, or a similar gathering. Having a responsibility accomplice offers outside help and consolation. Normal registrations permit you to share progress, examine difficulties, and celebrate victories. This outer responsibility supports your obligation to your aims.

11. **Energy Clearing Ceremonies:**
Integrate energy clearing ceremonies into your daily practice. This can incorporate practices, for example, smearing with sage, utilizing gems, or imagining a purifying light. These customs assist release with any negativing energy or blockages that might prevent the sign of your aims. As you participate in these ceremonies, center around relinquishing anything that no longer serves your objectives.

12. **Strengthening Explanations:**
Make a rundown of strengthening explanations that reverberate with your expectations. These assertions ought to summon a feeling of certainty, strength, and self-conviction. At the point when you experience self-uncertainty or difficulties, allude to your rundown of strengthening articulations to move your mentality and support your capacity to show your aims.

13. **Morning and Night Reflections:**
Toward the beginning of the day, set the vibe for your day by pondering your expectations. Avow your objectives, envision achievement, and offer thanks for the open doors that lie ahead. At night, audit your day, recognizing snapshots of arrangement with your aims and regions for development. This intelligent practice upgrades care and supports your obligation to your objectives.

14. **Careful Eating:**
Change supper time into a careful practice by mixing it with expectation. Prior to eating, pause for a minute to offer thanks for the sustenance. Set an expectation connected with your prosperity, for example, picking food varieties that invigorate and uphold your wellbeing. Careful eating interfaces your actual sustenance with your more extensive expectations for a solid and healthy lifestyle.

15. **Cleaning up and Space Arrangement:**
Clean actual mess off of your living and work areas to establish a climate that upholds your expectations. Mess can represent stale energy and prevent the progression of positive indications. As you clean up, set the aim for your space to mirror your objectives and yearnings. Orchestrate things deliberately, establishing an amicable and adjusted climate.

16. **Imaginative Articulation:**
Participate in imaginative exercises that permit you to communicate your aims outwardly or creatively. This could include painting, drawing, making, or some other type of imaginative articulation. Utilize this as a chance to externalize your objectives and feelings, making them unmistakable and supporting your obligation to their acknowledgment.

17. **Defining Limits:**
Lay out sound limits that line up with your expectations. This remembers

drawing certain lines for exercises or connections that channel your energy and cheapen your objectives. Clear limits make space for positive energy to stream, improving your capacity to keep on track and lined up with your goals.

18. **Intelligent Strolling or Nature Association:**
Join goal setting with active work by taking part in intelligent strolling or investing energy in nature. As you walk, center your psyche around your goals, permitting the cadenced development to improve your lucidity and focus. Nature association enhances the energy of your goals, encouraging a feeling of arrangement with the regular progression of life.

19. **Careful Innovation Use:**
Be purposeful about your utilization of innovation. Set the aim to utilize advanced gadgets carefully and deliberately. Make an offset that lines up with your objectives, limiting interruptions and enhancing the positive effect of innovation on your life. This exercise advances familiarity with how computerized collaborations add to or diminish your general prosperity.

20. **Intelligent Finish of-Day Audit:**

Close your day with an intelligent survey zeroed in on your expectations. Ask yourself inquiries, for example, What lined up with my expectations today? What difficulties did I face, and how could I explore them? What changes could I at any point make to more readily line up with my objectives tomorrow? This intelligent practice upgrades mindfulness and illuminates your way to deal with the forthcoming days.

Integrating these useful activities into your routine gives a comprehensive way to deal with aim setting and arrangement. Recollect that consistency and certified confidence in your capacity to show your aims are key parts of the cycle.

Explore different avenues regarding various activities, tailor them to suit your inclinations, and remain open to refining your aims as you advance on your excursion. By effectively captivating with these practices, you engage yourself to shape a reality that lines up with your most profound desires.

Chapter 5

The Morphing Mind in Society

The transforming mind in the public eye is a perplexing and many-sided peculiarity that envelops the powerful transaction between individual comprehension and the more extensive socio-social setting. In investigating the complexities of this cooperation, one should dig into the domains of brain research, social science, and neuroscience to disentangle the complicated strings that weave the texture of the human psyche inside the woven artwork of society.

At its center, the transforming mind is an idea that exemplifies the consistently changing nature of human cognizance. The psyche is certainly not a static element however a pliant and versatile organ that answers the bunch boosts present in the outside climate. This versatility is critical for endurance and progress in a world that is in a never-ending condition of motion.

Brain adaptability, a principal property of the cerebrum, underlines the transforming idea of the psyche. The cerebrum's capacity to rearrange itself in light of encounters, learning, and ecological requests is a demonstration of its dynamic nature. This versatility stretches out past the singular level and has significant ramifications for how social orders develop and deeply impact the personalities of their constituents.

Society, thus, goes about as a pot for the transforming mind. It gives the setting inside which people foster their mental cycles, convictions, and ways of behaving. From the snapshot of birth, people are drenched in a socio-social milieu that applies a significant effect on their psychological turn of events. The family, school system, media, and different social establishments add to molding the mental scene of people.

Family, as the essential social unit, assumes a crucial part in the beginning phases of mental turn of events. The communications inside the family set the establishment for a's comprehension singular might interpret connections, values, and normal practices. The transforming mind, in this way, starts its excursion inside the close bounds of familial connections, retaining social subtleties and social assumptions.

Schooling, as a formalized framework, further shapes the transforming mind. Schools act as pots of information transmission, where people obtain genuine data as well as incorporate cultural standards and values. The school system shapes mental cycles, imparts decisive reasoning abilities, and molds the manner in which people see themselves and their general surroundings.

The media, enveloping different structures like TV, the web, and print, is a strong power in the transforming of brains on a cultural scale. The media fills in as a mirror that reflects and shapes social stories, impacting popular assessment, and adding to the development of cultural standards. The steady blast of data from the media significantly affects individual viewpoints, molding convictions, mentalities, and, surprisingly, the actual texture of reality for some.

Social establishments, including strict associations, government structures, and financial frameworks, further add to the transforming mind in the public arena. These organizations give structures to grasping the world, laying out moral rules, and forming aggregate personality. The transforming mind is, subsequently, a singular peculiarity as well as an aggregate one, impacted by the more extensive socio-social environment.

In understanding the transforming mind, recognizing the job of social evolution is pivotal. Culture, characterized as the common convictions, values, and practices of a gathering, is a powerful power that shapes and is molded by the people inside it. The transmission of social data starting with one age then onto the next guarantees the congruity and transformation of cultural standards.

The transforming mind, impacted by social development, goes through shifts because of changing cultural elements. As social orders progress and experience new difficulties, the aggregate mentality advances to explore these intricacies. Mechanical progressions, globalization, and socio-political changes add to the consistent motion inside the transforming psyche of society.

The computerized age, portrayed by quick mechanical progressions and the expansion of data, has introduced another period in the transforming mind. The web, online entertainment, and advanced correspondence stages have reformed how data is scattered and consumed. This extraordinary admittance to data has suggestions for individual insight and cultural designs.

The computerized scene gives an abundance of data as well as difficulties customary thoughts of power and information. The democratization of data permits people to address laid out standards, participate in elective accounts, and partake in the co-making of information. The transforming mind, in the computerized age, is portrayed by a decentralization of impact, as people have more noteworthy organization in molding their mental scenes.

Notwithstanding, the advanced age likewise presents difficulties to the transforming mind. Data over-burden, the spread of deception, and the disintegration of security present huge worries. The steady barrage of boosts from computerized sources can prompt mental weakness and a divided identity. The transforming mind should explore the intricacies of the computerized scene while keeping an intelligible and strong mental construction.

The crossing point of the transforming psyche and innovation stretches out past data spread to incorporate the domain of computerized reasoning (artificial intelligence). As man-made intelligence frameworks become more coordinated into day to day existence, they add to the transforming mind in clever ways. Human-artificial intelligence associations, moral contemplations, and the effect of artificial intelligence on work and social designs all shape the developing mental scene of society.

The transforming mind is additionally affected by the financial designs that support society. Financial frameworks, whether industrialist, communist, or mixture, shape individual goals, values, and social progressive systems. Financial disparity, an unavoidable issue in numerous social orders, has significant ramifications for the transforming mind, impacting view of decency, equity, and the dissemination of assets.

Political philosophies and frameworks further add to the transforming mind in the public eye. The transaction between political power, administration designs, and individual opportunities shapes the shared mindset. Dictator systems might look to control and control the transforming mind through oversight, promulgation, and the concealment of dispute, while popularity based frameworks expect to encourage a climate of free articulation and various points of view.

The transforming mind in the public eye is definitely not a straight movement yet a unique exchange of different powers. It is molded by verifiable heritages, social practices, mechanical headways, and socio-political developments. The recurring pattern of cultural elements add to the ceaseless development of the transforming mind, mirroring the versatile idea of the two people and the shared perspective.

Social variety adds one more layer to the intricacy of the transforming mind. Various societies bring exceptional points of view, values, and perspectives to the worldwide woven artwork. The connection between different social components enhances the transforming mind, encouraging innovativeness, development, and a more extensive comprehension of the human experience.

Be that as it may, social variety can likewise prompt contentions and pressures as various perspectives impact. The transforming mind should explore the difficulties of social pluralism, tracking down ways of embracing variety while cultivating a feeling of shared mankind. In a globalized world, the transforming mind is interconnected, and the activities of one society swell across the more extensive human experience.

The transforming mind isn't just impacted by outside factors but at the same time is molded by inner cycles like feelings, recollections, and mental predispositions. Feelings assume a vital part in direction, social communications, and the development of significance. The transforming mind, in its personal aspect, mirrors the rhythmic movement of emotional encounters that variety individual and shared perspective.

Recollections, both individual and aggregate, add to the account of the transforming mind. Authentic occasions, social legacy, and shared recollections shape the manner in which people see themselves and their place in the public eye. The specific idea of memory, impacted by mental predispositions, adds to the development of stories that build up specific convictions and values.

Mental predispositions, intrinsic in human perspectives, likewise assume a huge part in the transforming mind. Tendency to look for predictable feedback, the inclination to look for data that lines up with existing convictions, and oblivious compliance, the adjustment to the assessments of a gathering, can impact decision-production at both individual and cultural levels. Perceiving and relieving these predispositions is urgent for cultivating a more nuanced and versatile transforming mind.

The idea of the transforming mind stretches out to the domain of social change and activism. Developments for social equality, orientation equity, natural equity, and other social causes mirror the aggregate undertaking to reshape the cultural scene. Activism is a sign of the transforming mind in real life, as people and networks challenge laid out standards, advocate for change, and endeavor to make a more even-handed and comprehensive society.

The transforming mind, with regards to activism, isn't just a reaction to outer treacheries yet in addition an impetus for cultural change. Grassroots developments, energized by the shared perspective, have the ability to challenge severe frameworks, rethink social stories, and prepare for an all the more and humane society. The transforming mind, through activism, turns into a main impetus for positive change.

Chasing understanding the transforming mind, the area of brain science assumes a focal part. Mental speculations, going from behaviorism to mental brain science to contemporary points of view on awareness, add to how we might interpret individual and aggregate mental cycles. The investigation of character, inspiration, and relational elements gives experiences into the variables that shape the transforming mind.

One unmistakable mental idea connected with the transforming mind is oneself. Oneself is a diverse develop that incorporates one's personality, convictions, values, and social jobs. The transforming mind, in its investigation of selfhood, wrestles with inquiries of realness, social assumptions, and the harmony among uniqueness and congruity. The development of self is a powerful cycle that unfurls inside the setting of social connections and social impacts.

Mental brain science, with its emphasis on mental cycles like insight, memory, and critical thinking, reveals insight into how the transforming mind explores the intricacies of data handling. The collaboration among cognizance and feeling, as concentrated on in fields like emotional neuroscience, gives a nuanced comprehension of the profound elements of the transforming mind.

The investigation of social brain research further clarifies the elements of the transforming mind with regards to relational connections, collective vibes, and cultural standards. Social impact, congruity, and bias are among the peculiarities that shape the shared awareness. The transforming mind, in its social aspect, mirrors the transaction of individual organization and the impact of the more extensive social setting.

Neuroscience, as a correlative field, offers bits of knowledge into the organic underpinnings of the transforming mind. Propels in cerebrum imaging advancements permit specialists to investigate the brain connects of mental cycles, feelings, and social associations. The multifaceted interconnections inside the cerebrum highlight the incorporated idea of the transforming mind, where mental and neurological elements unite.

The convergence of brain research, social science, and neuroscience gives an all encompassing structure to understanding the transforming mind in the public eye. An interdisciplinary undertaking perceives the association of individual cognizance and cultural designs. The transforming mind, as an idea, welcomes constant investigation and refinement as how we might interpret human instinct and cultural elements develops.

As the transforming mind explores the complicated landscape of the 21st 100 years, it faces uncommon difficulties and open doors. Worldwide emergencies, for example, environmental change, pandemics, and international contentions, highlight the interconnectedness of human social orders. The transforming mind should wrestle with the existential dangers presented by these difficulties while likewise outfitting the potential for aggregate activity and development.

The moral components of the transforming mind come to the cutting edge as mechanical headways bring up significant issues about security, independence, and the limits among human and man-made brainpower. As social orders embrace the advantages of mechanical advancement, moral contemplations become vital in guaranteeing that the transforming mind develops toward a path that lines up with human qualities and shields the prosperity of people and networks.

Schooling, as a key force to be reckoned with of the transforming mind, faces the basic to adjust to the changing necessities of a globalized and innovatively driven world. Educational plans should go past the transmission of genuine information to encourage decisive reasoning, the capacity to understand people on a profound level, and a feeling of worldwide citizenship. The transforming mind, in its instructive aspect, requires the development of abilities and mentalities that enable people to explore the intricacies of the cutting edge period.

The transforming mind additionally wrestles with issues of personality and portrayal. The acknowledgment of different voices, points of view, and encounters is fundamental for making a more comprehensive and fair society. The transforming mind, as its continued looking for credibility and having a place, stands up to the requirement for portrayal in media, schooling, and social stories.

All in all, the transforming mind in the public eye is a diverse and dynamic peculiarity that rises above individual perception to envelop the more extensive sociosocial setting. It is formed by a horde of variables, including family, instruction, media, innovation, financial matters, governmental issues, culture, and brain science. The exchange of these powers leads to a consistently advancing shared mindset that adjusts to the difficulties and chances of the contemporary world.

Understanding the transforming mind requires an interdisciplinary methodology that coordinates experiences from brain research, humanism, neuroscience, and different fields. It includes perceiving the complicated interconnections between individual mental cycles and the socio-social biological system. As the transforming mind keeps on exploring the intricacies of the 21st 100 years, it requires an insightful and moral commitment with the powers that shape human character and cultural elements.

5.1 Explore the collective consciousness and its influence on societal structures

The idea of the shared mindset is a hypothetical structure that dives into the common convictions, values, perspectives, and encounters that tight spot people inside a general public. It places that there exists a supply of shared information and understanding that rises above individual personalities, forming the character and elements of a gathering. To investigate the shared mindset and its effect on cultural designs, one should travel into the domains of social science, brain research, and social examinations, unwinding the complex strings that weave the woven artwork of human interconnectedness.

At its center, the shared perspective mirrors that people are not disengaged elements but rather interconnected creatures whose contemplations and ways of behaving are impacted by a common pool of social images and implications. The term was advocated by the French humanist Emile Durkheim, who contended that cultural attachment and request are kept up with through the presence of shared standards, values, and convictions that comprise the shared perspective. This common mental system goes about as a social paste, restricting people together and giving a feeling of having a place inside a local area.

Cultural designs, going from establishments to social practices, are profoundly interwoven with the shared awareness. Foundations, like family, training, religion, and government, assume a significant part in communicating and propagating the shared perspective across ages. They act as courses through which social qualities and standards are granted, molding the manner in which people see themselves and their jobs inside society.

Family, as the essential social unit, is a fundamental establishment that contributes essentially to the development of the shared mindset. Since early on, people are associated inside the family structure, retaining social standards, customs, and values. The family goes about as a microcosm of the more extensive society, engraving upon people the crucial components of the shared mindset that will impact their viewpoints and ways of behaving all through their lives.

Training, one more imperative establishment, fills in as a formalized framework for the transmission of information and social qualities. Schools bestow scholastic information as well as assume an essential part in forming the shared awareness by imparting cultural standards, virtues, and a mutual perspective of history and culture. The educational program, instructive methodologies, and school climate add to the embellishment of youthful personalities, impacting their perspective and their feeling of character inside the shared mindset.

Strict foundations, with their customs, lessons, and moral structures, are strong specialists in forming the shared mindset. Shared strict convictions give a feeling of motivation, significance, and moral direction for networks.

The shared mindset, as communicated through religion, encourages a common feeling of personality and having a place, impacting individual way of behaving as well as cultural designs and standards.

Government structures and political belief systems are additionally profoundly laced with the shared perspective. The predominant political framework, whether majority rule, dictator, communist, etc., mirrors the qualities and desires of the shared perspective. Political belief systems shape cultural designs, regulations, and arrangements, affecting the appropriation of force, assets, and valuable open doors inside the local area.

Media, as an unavoidable power in contemporary society, assumes a vital part in forming the shared perspective. The pictures, stories, and messages spread through different media channels add to the development of social images and implications. The media impacts general assessment, social perspectives, and, surprisingly, the development of reality itself, in this manner forming the shared mindset on a mass scale.

Social practices and customs, going from services to festivities, add to the encapsulation and support of the shared perspective. Divided social encounters make a feeling of solidarity and character between people inside a general public. These practices act as articulations of the shared perspective, building up friendly union and giving a system to shared significance making.

Language, as a principal component of human correspondence, is a critical transporter of the shared mindset. The words, images, and implications implanted in language mirror the social setting from which they arise. Through language, people convey and incorporate the qualities, standards, and shared encounters that comprise the shared perspective. Semantic articulations become a medium through which the shared mindset is explained and sustained.

Mentally, the shared perspective impacts individual cognizance and conduct through a cycle known as socialization. From earliest stages, people are associated into the standards and upsides of their social milieu. Socialization happens through direct collaborations with family, friends, and social establishments, as well as through roundabout impacts like media and social antiques. The assimilation of the shared mindset shapes people's discernments, perspectives, and dynamic cycles.

The shared mindset is definitely not a static element however a unique power that develops over the long run. Cultural changes, innovative progressions, and social movements add to the consistent change of the shared perspective. The interaction among congruity and change inside the shared mindset mirrors the versatility of social orders to new difficulties and valuable open doors.

Social advancement, driven by the intergenerational transmission of social data, guarantees the congruity and variation of the shared perspective. As social orders experience new conditions, whether through mechanical developments, globalization, or natural difficulties, the shared awareness goes through movements to oblige these changes. Social development is a unique interaction that shapes and is molded by the shared mindset.

The idea of the aggregate oblivious, presented by Swiss specialist Carl Jung, adds one more layer to the investigation of shared awareness. Jung suggested that there exists a layer of the oblivious brain shared by all individuals from a specific social or cultural gathering. This aggregate oblivious contains original images, pictures, and subjects that are acquired and reverberate across societies. The investigation of the aggregate oblivious gives bits of knowledge into the more deeply layers of the shared perspective that rise above individual encounters.

The shared perspective additionally crosses with the idea of personality, both individual and group. Character is an intricate interchange of individual and social factors that add to a singular's identity. The shared mindset impacts the development of individual personalities by giving social contents, standards, and assumptions. On the other hand, individual characters add to the variety and dynamism of the shared awareness.

Social attachment and soundness are intently attached to the strength and reverberation of the shared awareness. At the point when the shared mindset is vigorous and shared values are generally acknowledged, it encourages a feeling of having a place and solidarity inside a general public. Alternately, when there are cracks inside the shared mindset, emerging from social conflicts, social disparities, or clashing worth frameworks, it can prompt social disagreement and shakiness.

The development of social developments and activism mirrors the dynamism of the shared awareness in answering cultural difficulties. Developments for social equality, orientation correspondence, natural equity, and other social causes address aggregate endeavors to reshape the cultural scene. Activism is a sign of the shared mindset in real life, as people meet up to challenge laid out standards, advocate for change, and take a stab at an all the more and evenhanded society.

Globalization, with its interconnectedness and relationship, has significant ramifications for the shared perspective. The rising progression of data, social trade, and worldwide correspondence add to the hybridization of societies and the formation of a globalized shared perspective. Shared worldwide difficulties, for example, environmental change and pandemics, highlight the interconnected destiny of mankind and the requirement for an aggregate reaction.

Nonetheless, the globalized shared awareness isn't without its difficulties. Social homogenization, the strength of specific social stories, and the disintegration of neighborhood customs are concerns related with globalization. Finding some kind of harmony between the worldwide and the neighborhood is fundamental to keeping up with the extravagance and variety of the shared mindset in a globalized world.

The shared perspective likewise crosses with power elements inside society. The accounts and values implanted in the shared perspective can be controlled to serve the interests of people with great influence. Misleading publicity, restriction, and the control of data are apparatuses utilized by tyrant systems to shape and control the shared mindset in manners that merge power and stifle disagree.

In the period of data, the job of innovation in molding the shared awareness couldn't possibly be more significant. The web, online entertainment, and advanced correspondence stages have altered the spread of data and the arrangement of informal organizations. These innovations enhance the impact of the shared perspective on a worldwide scale, taking into consideration the fast spread of thoughts, social articulations, and shared encounters.

5.2 Discuss the role of cultural narratives in shaping societal norms

Social accounts act as strong courses through which social orders articulate, communicate, and sustain their qualities, convictions, and aggregate character. These accounts, containing stories, fantasies, images, and customs, assume a vital part in molding cultural standards — the common assumptions and rules that oversee individual conduct inside a local area. To dig into the job of social accounts in molding cultural standards, one should explore the complicated exchange between narrating, social personality, and the social development of the real world.

At its pith, a social account is a story that typifies the common encounters, values, and convictions of a specific local area. These accounts can take different structures, going from oral practices and composed writing to visual expressions, strict texts, and computerized media. The demonstration of narrating is imbued in human instinct, and social stories are the vessels through which networks figure out their past, present, and future.

Social stories act as a vault of aggregate memory, giving a system to grasping verifiable occasions, social starting points, and cultural changes. Through fantasies, legends, and verifiable records, social stories make a feeling of congruity and cognizance, interfacing people to their social legacy. The transmission of these stories from one age to another adds to the development of a common personality and a feeling of having a place inside a local area.

Cultural standards, as the unwritten principles that administer conduct and communication, are profoundly implanted in social accounts. These stories encode and build up the qualities considered significant by a general public, it is viewed as OK or no to direct what.

The ethical examples implanted in social stories shape the ethical compass of people, impacting their decisions, moral contemplations, and relational connections.

Strict texts are strong instances of social stories that significantly impact cultural standards. Across various societies and beliefs, hallowed sacred texts give profound direction as well as an ethical system for followers. The Ten Decrees in Judeo-Christian customs, for example, frame central moral rules that lastingly affect Western cultural standards. Likewise, the Quran in Islam and the Bhagavad Gita in Hinduism offer moral lessons that shape the way of behaving and upsides of their separate networks.

Scholarly works, from old stories to contemporary books, contribute essentially to the development of social accounts. Through narrating, creators investigate cultural subjects, scrutinize winning standards, and challenge laid out ideal models. Exemplary works, for example, George Orwell's "1984" or Chinua Achebe's "Things Self-destruct" have become piece of the social account, affecting points of view on power, administration, and social conflicts.

Social stories likewise manifest in the domain of legends and fantasies, frequently filling in as moral purposeful anecdotes that communicate cultural qualities to more youthful ages. The Siblings Grimm fantasies, for instance, are packed with moral illustrations and social themes that mirror the cultural standards of their time. These stories add to the socialization of people, ingraining social qualities and conduct assumptions since early on.

Visual expressions, including canvases, figures, and different types of visual narrating, assume a part in molding social stories. Through visual portrayal, craftsmen convey social images, authentic occasions, and cultural standards. For example, notable artworks like "Freedom Driving Individuals" by Eugène Delacroix or "Guernica" by Pablo Picasso act as visual accounts that catch verifiable minutes and cultural qualities.

In the advanced age, new types of narrating, like movies, TV, and online media, have arisen as powerful supporters of social accounts. The visual and hear-able nature of these mediums intensifies their effect, contacting different crowds and forming insights on a worldwide scale. Mainstream society, through motion pictures, television series, and web images, turns into a fundamental piece of the social account, affecting cultural standards and molding shared awareness.

Social accounts are not static; they advance and adjust to cultural changes, mirroring the dynamism of human societies. As social orders wrestle with shifts in values, mechanical headways, and international changes, social stories act as the two mirrors and engineers of cultural standards. The reevaluation of customary stories, the production of new accounts, and the contestation of existing standards add to the continuous development of social stories and the discussion of cultural standards.

One part of social accounts that altogether impacts cultural standards is the development of orientation jobs and assumptions. Customary stories frequently install orientation standards, supporting generalizations and molding cultural assumptions about manliness and womanliness. The maid in trouble saying or the chivalrous male model, for instance, can propagate orientation standards that might restrict individual articulation and valuable open doors.

On the other hand, social stories additionally have the ability to challenge and undermine laid out orientation standards. Contemporary writing, movies, and craftsmanship much of the time investigate elective accounts that question conventional orientation jobs, advance variety, and promoter for orientation equity. These stories add to cultural discussions about orientation, affecting discernments, and, after some time, adding to shifts in cultural standards.

The job of social stories in molding cultural standards stretches out to the domain of racial and ethnic personality. Authentic accounts, frequently implanted in social stories, can build up generalizations, sustain predispositions, and add to the underestimation of specific racial or ethnic gatherings. On the other hand, social stories can be an incredible asset for testing generalizations, recovering accounts, and encouraging a more comprehensive comprehension of different characters.

One model is the effect of writing and narrating in the African American experience. Stories, for example, those found in progress of Toni Morrison or Maya Angelou give a counter-story to verifiable persecution, offering a nuanced depiction of African American life, strength, and social wealth. These accounts challenge cultural standards established in bigotry and add to more extensive discussions about civil rights and fairness.

The worldwide interconnectedness worked with by current correspondence advances has prompted the rise of shared social accounts that rise above geographic limits. The web, virtual entertainment, and computerized stages empower the fast dispersal of social stories, making a globalized social scene. Shared stories, whether as images, viral recordings, or online developments, add to the arrangement of a worldwide social cognizance that impacts cultural standards across different networks.

Notwithstanding, the globalized idea of social accounts likewise brings up issues about social authority and the potential for the mastery of specific stories over others. The social accounts that gain unmistakable quality on the worldwide stage frequently mirror the viewpoints and upsides of strong countries or social gatherings. This dynamic can add to the homogenization of social accounts, eclipsing assorted voices and neighborhood viewpoints.

The impact of social stories on cultural standards isn't one-sided; it includes a corresponding relationship where cultural standards likewise shape the creation and gathering of social accounts.

Crowds bring their own social settings, encounters, and translations to the accounts they experience, affecting how these accounts are perceived and incorporated into the shared perspective.

Also, social stories can be locales of contestation and exchange, particularly in assorted and multicultural social orders. The conflict of social stories inside a general public mirrors the continuous exchange between various gatherings with particular qualities and perspectives. The exchange of social stories turns into a space where cultural standards are discussed, tested, and reclassified.

The job of social stories in molding cultural standards has significant ramifications for social change and activism. Accounts have the ability to assemble networks, rouse developments, and challenge abusive standards. Civil rights developments frequently influence narrating to bring issues to light, refine encounters, and promoter for change. The stories of underestimated gatherings, when enhanced and heard, become intense devices for reshaping cultural standards and cultivating a more comprehensive and evenhanded society.

Be that as it may, the extraordinary capability of social stories likewise experiences obstruction. Prevailing social accounts, particularly those imbued in authentic power structures, may oppose change and challenge to keep up with existing standards. Social accounts can become milestones where contending dreams of cultural standards conflict, reflecting more extensive battles for civil rights, fairness, and social portrayal.

All in all, the job of social stories in molding cultural standards is a dynamic and proportional cycle that impacts how people see, decipher, and explore their social universes. Social stories, whether sent through strict messages, writing, visual expressions, or computerized media, add to the development of aggregate personality, shared values, and moral systems inside a general public. Understanding this exchange between social stories and cultural standards is critical for grasping the mind boggling elements that shape human social orders and for cultivating discourse and inclusivity in an undeniably interconnected world.

5.3 Analyze how collective beliefs impact political, economic, and social realities

The nexus between aggregate convictions and the texture of political, financial, and social truths is a mind boggling exchange that characterizes the direction of social orders. Aggregate convictions, incorporating shared values, belief systems, and insights held by networks, use significant impact over the designs and elements of human development. To break down how aggregate convictions influence political, financial, and social real factors, one should investigate the corresponding connection between the outlook of a general public and the frameworks that oversee its association and working.

Political truths are profoundly laced with aggregate convictions, as they mirror the common belief systems and values that shape administration designs, strategies, and power elements inside a general public. Political frameworks, whether vote based, dictator, or some in the middle between, are based upon a groundwork of aggregate convictions that characterize the job of government, the conveyance of force, and the connection among residents and the state.

In just social orders, aggregate convictions about delegate administration, individual privileges, and law and order support the political framework. The confidence in the authenticity of chosen delegates, the significance of city cooperation, and the assurance of central freedoms shapes the bedrock of popularity based administration. The aggregate confidence in the standard of one individual, one vote shapes political support and dynamic cycles, impacting the choice of pioneers and the plan of arrangements.

Tyrant systems, then again, frequently draw upon aggregate convictions that focus on hand, security, and concentrated power. The political reality in such frameworks is shaped by the aggregate acknowledgment of various leveled power structures, restricted political opportunities, and a faith in the need areas of strength for of administration. The aggregate faith in the power of the state and the subjection of individual freedoms to the general benefit of the country shapes political practices, strategies, and the dispersion of assets.

Political philosophies, which are signs of aggregate convictions about the best cultural request, assume an essential part in forming political real factors. Whether grounded in traditionalism, radicalism, communism, or other philosophical structures, these aggregate convictions impact strategy choices, party stages, and the general course of political plans. The recurring pattern of political philosophies mirror the developing shared mindset of a general public and add to the molding of political real factors after some time.

Monetary real factors, from the designs of creation and dispersion to examples of abundance and neediness, are significantly affected by aggregate convictions about the idea of financial frameworks and the job of people inside them. Monetary philosophies, like free enterprise, communism, or blended market economies, are impressions of aggregate convictions about the most fair and proficient method for putting together financial exercises.

In industrialist social orders, the predominant aggregate conviction frequently bases on the standards of unrestricted economy rivalry, confidential property freedoms, and individual business venture. This conviction framework shapes financial designs that focus on market influences, benefit motivators, and the collection of abundance as main thrusts for monetary development. The truth of free enterprise is set apart by the quest for personal responsibility, market-driven asset portion, and differing levels of pay disparity.

Conversely, communist economies are supported by aggregate convictions in the significance of aggregate possession, social government assistance, and the decrease of financial abberations. The monetary reality in communist frameworks mirrors a promise to the arrangement of public products, state mediation in financial exercises, and endeavors to relieve class-based imbalances. The aggregate faith in friendly value and the requirement for state mediation shapes financial approaches, abundance conveyance systems, and social security nets.

The connection between aggregate convictions and monetary truths isn't restricted to the polarity of private enterprise and communism. Numerous social orders take on blended market economies that mix components of both, reflecting nuanced aggregate convictions about the job of government, market influences, and social obligation. The financial real factors in these frameworks mirror a continuous discussion between different aggregate convictions, bringing about half breed models that try to adjust contending values.

The effect of aggregate convictions on monetary real factors stretches out past the macroeconomic level to individual ways of behaving and direction. Buyer ways of behaving, venture examples, and work market elements are impacted by aggregate convictions about progress, riches, and the quest for joy. The aggregate confidence in the worth of commercialization, for instance, fills request driven economies, while the faith in the nobility of work shapes the elements of the labor force.

Social real factors, including social standards, relational connections, and personality builds, are significantly molded by aggregate convictions about what is considered OK, attractive, or untouchable inside a general public. Social stories, communicated through customs, training, and media, add to the arrangement of aggregate convictions that impact normal practices and assumptions.

Aggregate convictions about orientation, for example, influence social real factors by molding assumptions about jobs, ways of behaving, and open doors for people. Cultural standards encompassing family designs, marriage, and nurturing are profoundly implanted in aggregate convictions about orientation jobs. The effect of these convictions is reflected in friendly practices, arrangements, and the conveyance of chances and assets in light of orientation.

Convictions about race and nationality likewise add to social real factors, impacting examples of consideration, rejection, and segregation inside a general public. Aggregate convictions about racial predominance or inadequacy, sustained through verifiable accounts, social images, and fundamental designs, shape the lived encounters of people and networks. Social imbalances, abberations in admittance to schooling, business, and equity, are in many cases signs of profoundly imbued aggregate convictions about race.

Strict convictions, one more critical component of aggregate conviction frameworks, assume a focal part in molding social real factors. The ethical structures, moral rules, and social practices related with strict convictions add to the development of cultural standards. Aggregate convictions about profound quality, equity, and the reason for life, frequently established in strict customs, impact social ways of behaving, general sets of laws, and moral principles inside a local area.

The effect of aggregate convictions on friendly truths is especially obvious in the domain of profound quality and morals. Cultural standards with respect to genuineness, trustworthiness, and benevolence are profoundly affected by aggregate convictions about what is thought of as prudent or condemnable. The acknowledgment or dismissal of specific ways of behaving inside a general public is many times dependent upon aggregate convictions about ethical quality, which, thusly, shape legitimate systems, social assumptions, and relational connections.

Political, financial, and social truths are not autonomous circles but rather are complicatedly interconnected, each affecting and being impacted by the others. Aggregate convictions act as the connective tissue that winds around these aspects together, impacting the standards, values, and establishments that portray a general public. The corresponding connection between aggregate convictions and these real factors makes a dynamic and developing social scene.

The flexibility of aggregate convictions and their effect on cultural designs highlight the potential for social change and change. Aggregate convictions are not fixed; they can be challenged, reworked, and reshaped through discourse, schooling, and aggregate activity. Social developments, activism, and support endeavors frequently arise as articulations of elective aggregate convictions that challenge existing standards and try to rethink political, monetary, and social real factors.

Be that as it may, the groundbreaking capability of aggregate convictions additionally experiences obstruction, especially when profoundly dug in convictions are connected to existing power structures. Political, monetary, and social frameworks that are lined up with specific aggregate convictions might oppose change, prompting strains between those looking for change and those put resources into keeping up with the norm. The battle for social change becomes, to some extent, a battle for the reshaping of aggregate convictions that support cultural designs.

Chapter 6

The Psychology of Change

Change is an inborn and unavoidable part of the human experience, complicatedly woven into the texture of our lives. From the second we are conceived, we go through a constant course of development and change, both on a physical and mental level. The capacity to adjust to change is a crucial quality of human instinct, but, the brain science of progress is a perplexing and diverse peculiarity that has charmed researchers, clinicians, and thinkers from the beginning of time.

At its center, the brain science of progress digs into the multifaceted operations of the human psyche and investigates the variables that impact our reactions to different life changing occasions. It envelops a wide range of encounters, going from self-improvement and self-disclosure to significant life changes and cultural changes. Understanding the mental underpinnings of progress is essential for individual prosperity as well as for exploring the difficulties of an always developing world.

One of the vital components in understanding the brain science of progress is perceiving that people are innately predictable animals. The solace and security given by recognizable schedules and examples make a feeling of solidness in our lives. These propensities, whether cognizant or oblivious, act as mental anchors that ground us amidst vulnerability. Thusly, when confronted with the possibility of progress, people frequently experience a scope of feelings, including nervousness, dread, and obstruction.

The feeling of dread toward the obscure is profoundly imbued in the human mind, setting off a base sense for self-safeguarding. Change upsets the harmony of our laid out schedules, compelling us to go up against new regions and step outside our usual ranges of familiarity. This inconvenience can be a strong obstacle, convincing people to oppose change in any event, when it very well might be useful or essential for self-awareness.

The mental protection from change is a proven and factual peculiarity in different fields, including hierarchical brain science, where specialists and experts wrestle with the difficulties of carrying out change inside organizations and foundations. Representatives might oppose hierarchical changes because of worries about professional stability, apprehension about the obscure, or an apparent danger to their capability and skill. Perceiving and tending to these mental hindrances is urgent for effective change the board drives.

Notwithstanding outside factors, interior mental cycles assume a critical part in forming our reactions to change. The mental and close to home parts of the human brain are profoundly interconnected, impacting our discernments, perspectives, and ways of behaving. Mental discord, a hypothesis presented by clinician Leon Festinger, features the inconvenience that emerges when people hold clashing convictions or perspectives. When faced with change, individuals might encounter mental disharmony as they accommodate their current convictions with the new reality, prompting a scope of profound reactions.

The most common way of adjusting to change includes mental rebuilding as well as close to home guideline. Feelings act as strong marks of our inner states, flagging our responses to outer boosts. The close to home rollercoaster related with change can envelop a wide range, from the underlying shock or disavowal to inevitable acknowledgment and transformation. Understanding and exploring these profound elements are fundamental for encouraging strength and advancing mental prosperity during seasons of progress.

In addition, the brain research of progress reaches out past individual encounters to envelop cultural and social aspects. The aggregate mind of a general public shapes its ability to embrace or oppose change for a bigger scope. Social standards, customs, and authentic inheritances impact the manner in which networks see and explore extraordinary cycles. Cultural change frequently ignites banters about personality, values, and the circulation of force, mirroring the multifaceted transaction among individual and aggregate brain science.

The appearance of mechanical progressions and the globalization of data have sped up the speed of cultural change, presenting remarkable difficulties and amazing open doors. The computerized age has altered correspondence, business, and social associations, reshaping the texture of human culture. The mental effect of these fast cultural changes is a subject of continuous examination, with researchers inspecting the ramifications for emotional well-being, relational connections, and social character.

With regards to globalization, the interconnectedness of different societies has led to a worldwide cognizance that rises above conventional limits. The brain research of progress in a globalized world includes exploring the pressures between social variety and the general human experience. As people and social orders wrestle with the ramifications of a quickly impacting world, encouraging social insight and intercultural understanding becomes basic for advancing concordance and cooperation.

Inside the domain of self-awareness, the brain science of progress assumes a critical part in the excursion of self-revelation and satisfaction. Individuals have an inborn drive for development and realization, trying to understand their maximum capacity. The course of self-revelation includes thoughtfulness, self-reflection, and an eagerness to embrace change as an impetus for individual change.

Clinician Abraham Maslow's progressive system of requirements gives a structure to figuring out the inspirational elements that drive human way of behaving. At the zenith of the order is self-completion, addressing the acknowledgment of one's special potential and capacities. The quest for self-completion involves a consistent excursion of personal growth and variation to new encounters, showing the inherent connection between self-improvement and the brain research of progress.

In the domain of psychotherapy, the brain science of progress is a focal concentration, as specialists work cooperatively with clients to explore the difficulties of change. The helpful cycle includes investigating firmly established convictions, testing maladaptive examples, and working with the advancement of survival techniques. Whether resolving issues of injury, compulsion, or self-awareness, specialists perceive the groundbreaking force of progress in the mending system.

The idea of strength is vital to understanding how people explore misfortune and return quickly from life's difficulties. Flexibility isn't just the shortfall of misery however the ability to adjust, develop, and flourish despite affliction. The brain research of flexibility envelops mental, profound, and conduct angles, featuring the job of outlook in forming one's reaction to troublesome conditions.

Research in sure brain science has revealed insight into the variables that add to versatility, underscoring the significance of good faith, social help, and a feeling of direction. The capacity to reexamine difficulties as any open doors for development is a sign of versatile people, highlighting the groundbreaking expected innate in the brain science of progress.

According to a neurobiological point of view, the cerebrum's pliancy, or capacity to redesign itself, highlights the neurobiological premise of progress. Brain adaptability empowers the cerebrum to adjust and frame new brain associations because of encounters and ecological upgrades. This powerful exchange between the mind and conduct gives a logical establishment to grasping how mediations, like treatment or growth opportunities, can prompt enduring changes in brain processes.

The field of positive brain adaptability investigates how deliberate practices, like care and reflection, can emphatically influence the mind's design and capability. These practices have been related with expanded dark matter thickness in regions connected with mindfulness, empathy, and profound guideline. The neurobiological bits of knowledge into the brain research of progress offer a comprehensive comprehension of the psyche body association and the potential for deliberate intercessions to shape brain engineering.

The idea of progress additionally includes conspicuously in the area of instructive brain research, where researchers and teachers investigate how understudies learn and adjust to new data. The brain research of learning is unpredictably connected to the course of mental turn of events, as people absorb new information, abilities, and viewpoints. Instructive speculations, for example, Jean Piaget's phases of mental turn of events, feature the job of mental designs in molding growth opportunities.

In the advanced age, the scene of schooling is going through huge changes, with web based learning, virtual homerooms, and intuitive advancements becoming necessary parts of the instructive cycle. The brain research of progress in training reaches out past educational techniques to envelop the social and close to home components of learning. Cultivating a development outlook, advancing capacity to understand people at their core, and adjusting instructing systems to different learning styles are fundamental for planning understudies to flourish in a steadily impacting world.

The working environment addresses one more field where the brain research of progress is a basic figure individual and hierarchical achievement. In the present dynamic and serious business climate, associations should explore steady mechanical progressions, market changes, and developing buyer inclinations. The capacity to adjust to change is an essential basic for organizations looking to flourish in an undeniably unpredictable and questionable scene.

Authoritative analysts concentrate on the elements of progress inside the work environment, inspecting factors that work with or ruin fruitful hierarchical change drives. The job of administration, correspondence, and hierarchical culture in forming representatives' mentalities toward change is a point of convergence of exploration in this field. Viable change the executives techniques require a nuanced comprehension of the mental variables that impact representative commitment, inspiration, and obligation to hierarchical objectives.

The brain science of progress is likewise interlaced with the idea of inspiration, a main impetus that drives people to seek after objectives and beat obstructions. Inspiration includes both inborn and outward factors, mirroring the interaction between private qualities, goals, and outside remunerations. Understanding the brain science of inspiration is fundamental for instructors, businesses, and people looking to improve execution and make progress.

The Self-Assurance Hypothesis (SDT), created by Edward Deci and Richard Ryan, gives a structure to figuring out the various sorts of inspiration and their effect on conduct. SDT recognizes three fundamental mental necessities — independence, ability, and relatedness — that, when fulfilled, add to inherent inspiration and prosperity. The use of SDT in different areas, including schooling, work, and medical services, features the widespread importance of inspiration in working with positive results.

In the domain of wellbeing brain research, the brain research of progress assumes a urgent part in tending to conduct change and advancing prosperity. Wellbeing ways of behaving, like eating regimen, exercise, and adherence to clinical medicines, are frequently difficult to alter because of the mind boggling interaction of mental, social, and natural variables. Mediations pointed toward advancing wellbeing conduct change influence standards from social brain research, mental social treatment, and inspirational talking.

The Transtheoretical Model (TTM), created by James Prochaska and Carlo DiClemente, gives a system to understanding the phases of conduct change. The model sets that people travel through unmistakable stages — precontemplation, examination, readiness, activity, support, and end — on their excursion toward conduct change. Fitting mediations to people's status for change is a vital standard of the TTM, underlining the significance of customized approaches in advancing supported conduct change.

The brain science of progress is additionally fundamental to grasping enslavement and recuperation. Substance use problems include an intricate exchange of hereditary, mental, and ecological variables, adding to the constant idea of habit. The phases of progress model, got from the TTM, has been applied to the field of fixation treatment, perceiving that people progress through various phases of status for change in their recuperation process.

Habit treatment draws near, for example, inspirational upgrade treatment and mental social treatment, integrate standards from the brain research of progress to address the hidden variables adding to habit-forming ways of behaving. The acknowledgment of fixation as a persistent, backsliding condition highlights the significance of progressing backing and intercessions that adjust to people's developing requirements.

In the more extensive setting of cultural change, the brain science of social developments gives experiences into the elements of aggregate activity and social change. Social developments, whether supporting for social equality, natural equity, or orientation fairness, are powered by the aggregate goals of people looking for change on a cultural level. The brain science of social change investigates the inspirations, personalities, and overall vibes that drive people to partake in and support social developments.

Clinician Gustave Le Bon's work on swarm brain science and social personality hypothesis add to how we might interpret what people's way of behaving and mentalities can be meant for inside a gathering setting. The mental components that underlie social developments, like shared character, aggregate adequacy, and moral outlining, shed light on the elements that add to the achievement or disappointment of extraordinary cultural drives.

The convergence of brain research and natural supportability highlights the dire requirement for aggregate activity to address worldwide difficulties, for example, environmental change. The brain research of natural way of behaving analyzes the elements that impact people's perspectives and ways of behaving toward the climate, investigating roads for advancing supportable practices and moderating biological effect.

Conduct intercessions informed by mental standards, for example, poking and normal practice mediations, expect to energize supportive of ecological ways of behaving for an enormous scope. Understanding the brain research of progress with regards to ecological supportability is critical for cultivating a feeling of aggregate liability and elevating ways of behaving that add to the prosperity of the planet.

All in all, the brain science of progress is an immense and interdisciplinary field that traverses individual, relational, hierarchical, and cultural aspects. Change is an innate part of the human experience, molding our turn of events, affecting our connections, and driving cultural changes. The mental cycles that underlie our reactions to change are mind boggling, including mental, profound, and conduct elements.

Whether with regards to self-awareness, hierarchical change, or cultural developments, understanding the brain science of progress is fundamental for exploring the difficulties and valuable open doors that emerge in a consistently advancing world.

The mix of experiences from neuroscience, positive brain research, hierarchical brain research, and different disciplines gives a thorough system to investigating the complexities of the human psyche even with change.

As people and social orders keep on wrestling with the intricacies of a quickly impacting world, the brain science of progress fills in as a compass, directing us through the strange domains of change. Embracing the intrinsic potential for development and transformation permits us to get by as well as flourish despite vulnerability, encouraging strength, prosperity, and an aggregate limit with respect to positive change.

6.1 Examine the resistance to change and the fear of the unknown

The protection from change and the apprehension about the obscure address profoundly imbued parts of human brain science that impact how people and associations explore groundbreaking cycles. Change, by its actual nature, disturbs laid out schedules and presents vulnerability, setting off close to home reactions that reach from trepidation to altogether obstruction. This obstruction is established in a complicated exchange of mental, profound, and social elements, mirroring a crucial pressure between the solace of commonality and the difficulties presented by the new.

At its center, the feeling of dread toward the obscure is a basic intuition that has developmental roots. All through mankind's set of experiences, the obscure frequently likened to expected dangers, inciting people to move toward new circumstances with alert. This instinctual reaction is profoundly implanted in the human mind, and it appears in different structures when faced with change, be it individual, proficient, or cultural.

The mental protection from change is a proven and factual peculiarity, and various speculations have tried to explain its fundamental components. One noticeable hypothesis is Kurt Lewin's Change The executives Model, which distinguishes three phases: thawing, changing, and refreezing. Thawing includes breaking down existing outlooks and making a mental status for change. Be that as it may, opposition can arise during this stage as people wrestle with the distress of relinquishing natural examples.

The mental uneasiness related with change is much of the time exacerbated by a mental peculiarity known as mental cacophony. This hypothesis, created by Leon Festinger, places that people experience mental uneasiness while holding clashing convictions or perspectives. When faced with change, mental cacophony emerges as people accommodate their current convictions with the new reality, prompting close to home and mental conflict.

In the hierarchical setting, the protection from change is an unavoidable test that influences workers and pioneers the same. Hierarchical change, whether it includes rebuilding, new innovation executions, or changes in corporate culture, frequently meets with opposition from representatives who see it as a danger to their dependability and capability.

The apprehension about employment cutback, vulnerability about new jobs and obligations, and worries about their capacity to adjust add to this opposition.

Initiative assumes an essential part in overseeing protection from change inside associations. Compelling correspondence, straightforwardness, and including representatives in the dynamic cycle can relieve fears and encourage a feeling of pride in the change interaction. Notwithstanding, an absence of clear correspondence, lacking help, or an apparent negligence for workers' interests can heighten opposition and obstruct the outcome of hierarchical change drives.

Understanding the mental elements of protection from change is fundamental for pioneers trying to effectively explore complex authoritative changes. Perceiving that opposition is a characteristic reaction to the new permits pioneers to address concerns proactively, encouraging a culture that values versatility and strength.

On a singular level, the anxiety toward the obscure can appear as uneasiness, misgiving, or a hesitance to embrace new open doors. Whether it's leaving on another vocation way, moving to an alternate city, or undertaking an individual change, people frequently wrestle with the vulnerability that goes with change. The feeling of dread toward the obscure can be deadening, impeding self-awareness and keeping people from understanding their maximum capacity.

Analysts and advisors frequently work with people to investigate and comprehend the underlying drivers of their apprehension about the unexplored world. Mental conduct treatment (CBT) is a generally utilized restorative methodology that helps people distinguish and challenge pessimistic idea designs adding to uneasiness and opposition. By rethinking discernments and creating survival techniques, people can construct flexibility and explore the obscure no sweat.

In addition, the apprehension about the obscure can be connected to more extensive existential worries. The rationalist Søren Kierkegaard investigated the idea of existential nervousness, which emerges from the attention to life's vulnerabilities and the intrinsic opportunity to decide. Embracing this existential opportunity includes standing up to the obscure and going with choices notwithstanding the intrinsic dangers, a cycle that requires fortitude and self-reflection.

Existential clinicians, like Viktor Frankl and Rollo May, have stressed the significance of tracking down importance and reason notwithstanding life's vulnerabilities. The apprehension about the obscure turns into an impetus for self-revelation and self-improvement when people participate in a quest for importance, rising above prompt uneasiness to seek after more profound, additional satisfying parts of their lives.

In the domain of neuroscience, the apprehension about the obscure is related with the cerebrum's repugnance for vulnerability. The mind, as a prescient organ, looks to limit vulnerability and foresee future occasions to guarantee endurance. Vulnerability initiates the amygdala, the cerebrum's personal community, setting off a pressure reaction. This brain system is well established in developmental history, where the capacity to expect and answer potential dangers was essential for endurance.

Understanding the neurobiological premise of the feeling of dread toward the obscure gives bits of knowledge into why people might encounter elevated nervousness when gone up against with vulnerability. Care practices and mediations that advance acknowledgment of vulnerability have shown guarantee in relieving the brain and mental reactions related with the anxiety toward the unexplored world.

With regards to cultural and social change, the feeling of dread toward the obscure can appear on an aggregate level. Social orders, similar to people, may oppose change because of worries about the expected results on social character, social union, and laid out standards. Social anthropologist Clifford Geertz's idea of "social involution" investigates how social orders might oppose outer impacts and changes that challenge their conventional lifestyles.

The apprehension about social digestion and the disintegration of social legacy can lead networks to oppose globalization and modernization endeavors. This obstruction is much of the time grounded in a craving to protect exceptional social personalities and keep a feeling of congruity across ages. Adjusting the advantages of progress with the safeguarding of social legacy turns into a sensitive errand for social orders exploring the intricacies of worldwide change.

Political and monetary changes at the cultural level can likewise summon dread of the unexplored world. The destroying of laid out political frameworks, financial changes, or changes in administration might be met with obstruction from people and gatherings acclimated with the strength given by existing designs. Understanding and tending to these apprehensions is fundamental for cultivating valuable discourse and cooperation chasing after sure cultural changes.

The feeling of dread toward the obscure is a repetitive topic in writing, reasoning, and craftsmanship. Artistic works frequently investigate characters' excursions through strange domains, featuring the extraordinary capability of standing up to the unexplored world. Joseph Campbell's idea of the "legend's excursion" highlights the model account of people confronting and beating the obscure, arising more grounded and savvier.

In workmanship and reasoning, the obscure is many times depicted as a well-spring of motivation and imagination. Rationalist Martin Heidegger suggested that embracing the obscure permits people to encounter certified snapshots of realness and opportunity.

The idea of the great in craftsmanship, as expressed by masterminds like Immanuel Kant, stresses the sensational idea of the obscure and its ability to bring out significant close to home and stylish encounters.

The feeling of dread toward the obscure is likewise investigated in the field of direction and hazard discernment. Conduct financial matters and brain science have shown that people might display silly ways of behaving when confronted with dubious results. Prospect hypothesis, created by Daniel Kahneman and Amos Tversky, investigates how people weigh expected misfortunes and gains in navigation, showing that individuals are more unwilling to misfortunes than they are roused by comparable additions.

Risk discernment is intrinsically attached to the apprehension about the obscure, as people evaluate the possible outcomes of their choices. The exchange between mental predispositions, close to home reactions, and chance discernment highlights the intricacy of dynamic in questionable circumstances. Perceiving these mental and close to home variables is significant for policymakers, teachers, and people trying to settle on educated choices in the face regarding vulnerability.

Conquering the feeling of dread toward the obscure requires a diverse methodology that addresses mental, profound, and cultural aspects. Fostering a development outlook, as proposed by therapist Hymn Dweck, includes seeing difficulties as any open doors for learning and development instead of unrealistic deterrents. This mentality shift can enable people to move toward the obscure with interest and strength.

Care rehearses, established in customs, for example, Buddhism, offer devices for developing mindfulness and acknowledgment of the current second, including its vulnerabilities. Care urges people to notice their contemplations and feelings without judgment, advancing a non-receptive and liberal way to deal with the unexplored world. Research has demonstrated the way that care mediations can lessen uneasiness and work on prosperity by changing brain processes related with dread and stress.

6.2 Discuss psychological strategies for embracing change and fostering personal growth

Embracing change and encouraging self-awareness are interlaced cycles that include a mix of mental procedures pointed toward beating opposition, developing flexibility, and advancing positive change. As people explore the intricacies of life, they experience different changes, both expected and unforeseen, that require versatile reactions. Understanding and executing mental systems can engage people to adapt to change as well as flourish even with vulnerability.

One essential mental methodology for embracing change is developing a development outlook. Instituted by therapist Song Dweck, a development outlook includes seeing difficulties and misfortunes as any open doors for learning and improvement as opposed to fixed marks of one's capacities. People with a development outlook accept that their insight and capacities can be created through devotion, exertion, and gaining from encounters.

Developing a development mentality starts with mindfulness and the acknowledgment that one's convictions about insight and ability can shape their reactions to challenges. By rethinking disappointments as any open doors to learn and improve, people with a development outlook are bound to embrace change with a feeling of interest and strength. This mental system works with versatility as well as encourages an uplifting outlook towards self-awareness.

Care rehearses address one more impressive mental procedure for exploring change and encouraging self-improvement. Established in thoughtful practices, for example, Buddhism, care includes developing attention to the current second without judgment. Care works on, including reflection and careful breathing, assist people with fostering a non-responsive and liberal way to deal with their viewpoints and feelings.

Research in brain science and neuroscience has shown the positive effect of care on mental prosperity. Customary care practice has been related with diminished pressure, worked on close to home guideline, and improved mental adaptability — credits that are especially significant despite change. By developing care, people can foster a more prominent ability to explore vulnerability, oversee pressure, and cultivate self-awareness.

Positive brain science mediations offer a third mental methodology for embracing change and cultivating self-improvement. Positive brain research, a field spearheaded by Martin Seligman, centers around developing qualities and temperances to improve by and large prosperity. Intercessions, for example, appreciation journaling, qualities recognizable proof, and positive insistences can move people's concentration toward their assets and achievements, encouraging a positive outlook.

Appreciation journaling, for instance, includes consistently recording things one is grateful for. This training has been connected to expanded life fulfillment and positive feelings. Likewise, distinguishing and using individual qualities in different life spaces can upgrade self-viability and flexibility, elevating a proactive way to deal with change. Positive confirmations, when rehearsed truly, can add to molding a positive mental self view and outlook helpful for self-awareness.

In the domain of psychotherapy, mental conduct approaches give viable mental systems to embracing change and encouraging self-awareness. Mental social treatment (CBT) is an objective situated remedial methodology that helps people recognize and challenge maladaptive idea examples and ways of behaving.

By reexamining negative contemplations and carrying out sure conduct changes, people can foster survival strategies and strength despite life's difficulties.

CBT mediations frequently incorporate mental rebuilding, where people figure out how to distinguish and challenge nonsensical convictions that add to gloomy feelings. This cycle includes supplanting contorted contemplations with additional decent and valuable ones. Moreover, social mediations, for example, openness treatment, help people go up against and conquer fears, working with self-improvement and versatile reactions to change.

Building the capacity to understand anyone on a profound level addresses one more mental system fundamental for exploring change and encouraging self-awareness. The ability to appreciate individuals on a deeper level includes perceiving, understanding, and dealing with one's own feelings, as well as relating to the feelings of others. People with high ability to appreciate individuals on a profound level are better prepared to explore relational connections, adjust to evolving conditions, and settle on informed choices.

Creating the capacity to understand individuals on a deeper level requires self-reflection and a pledge to grasping the profound parts of one's encounters. Practices, for example, journaling, looking for criticism from others, and participating in sympathetic correspondence add to the advancement of the capacity to understand people on a deeper level. This mental system not just upgrades people's capacity to adapt to change yet in addition encourages significant associations and self-improvement in different parts of life.

With regards to hierarchical brain science, mental wellbeing is a vital system for cultivating self-awareness and embracing change inside working environment settings. Mental security alludes to the discernment that one can communicate their thoughts, face challenges, and commit errors unafraid of adverse results. In mentally safe conditions, people feel engaged to add to advancement, share different viewpoints, and adjust to hierarchical changes.

Initiative assumes a critical part in laying out and keeping up with mental wellbeing inside associations. Pioneers who cultivate a comprehensive and strong culture urge representatives to voice their perspectives and proceed with potentially dangerous courses of action. This, thus, establishes a climate where people feel esteemed, adding to their own and proficient development. Mental wellbeing is especially significant with regards to authoritative change, as it works with open correspondence and cooperation.

Story treatment offers a novel mental methodology that spotlights on people's accounts and the development of significance in their lives. Created by Michael White and David Epston, account treatment includes investigating and reshaping the narratives people tell about themselves and their encounters. By reexamining accounts and recognizing individual organization, people can make engaging stories that work with self-improvement and flexibility despite change.

Account treatment includes externalizing issues, isolating them from one's character, and cooperatively recreating elective stories. This cycle permits people to see difficulties as outer powers that can be tended to, as opposed to inborn parts of their character. By reshaping their stories, people can embrace change as a continuous course of self-improvement and change.

Objective laying out and objective situated procedures address crucial mental methodologies for encouraging self-improvement and exploring change. Setting clear, feasible objectives gives people an internal compass and inspiration. Whether present moment or long haul, objectives act as persuasive benchmarks that guide conduct and elevate a proactive way to deal with change.

The Savvy models — Explicit, Quantifiable, Feasible, Significant, and Time-bound — offer an organized structure for objective setting. Separating bigger objectives into more modest, sensible advances improves people's capacity to follow progress and celebrate accomplishments en route. Objective situated techniques add to self-awareness as well as give a guide to exploring the intricacies of progress with reason and expectation.

Social help and relational connections comprise a urgent mental technique for exploring change and encouraging self-improvement. Individuals are innately friendly animals, and the nature of social associations significantly impacts psychological wellness and prosperity. Positive connections offer profound help, support, and a feeling of having a place, which are fundamental for strength despite change.

Creating and keeping up with social associations includes both giving and getting support. Effectively searching out friendly communications, sharing encounters, and communicating weakness add to the strength of relational securities. Moreover, offering help to others cultivates a feeling of direction and correspondence. Social encouraging groups of people act as mainstays of versatility, assisting people with enduring the difficulties of progress and advancing self-improvement through shared encounters.

Self-sympathy, as proposed by therapist Kristin Neff, offers an empathetic and non-critical way to deal with oneself, particularly in the midst of trouble or disappointment. Self-sympathy includes treating oneself with the very graciousness and understanding that one would propose to a companion confronting comparable difficulties. This mental system is especially important while exploring change, as it mitigates self-analysis and encourages a positive and supporting interior discourse.

Rehearsing self-sympathy incorporates recognizing and approving one's feelings, perceiving the common human experience of confronting difficulties, and rethinking pessimistic self-talk. By embracing self-sympathy, people can develop versatility and foster a more adjusted viewpoint on change, recognizing that mishaps are a characteristic piece of the human experience and a chance for development.

A development situated mentality, care rehearses, positive brain research mediations, mental conduct draws near, the capacity to understand people at their core improvement, mental security in associations, story treatment, objective situated techniques, social help, and self-sympathy are interconnected mental procedures that by and large enable people to embrace change.

6.3 Explore the concept of resilience and adaptability in morphing minds

The idea of strength and versatility in transforming minds digs into the dynamic and advancing nature of the human mind. Strength, frequently portrayed as the capacity to return from affliction, and flexibility, the ability to conform to new conditions, are interconnected characteristics that shape how people explore life's difficulties and changes. Understanding the mental systems that add to flexibility and versatility is fundamental for appreciating the intricacies of human way of behaving and encouraging mental prosperity.

Strength isn't just the shortfall of pain yet the capacity to flourish and fill even with misfortune. The underlying foundations of strength are in many cases followed back to formative encounters, including early connections, methods for dealing with hardship or stress, and openness to difficulty. The spearheading work of analysts like Emmy Werner and Michael Rutter established the groundwork for the investigation of strength by looking at people who, regardless of confronting huge dangers and difficulties, showed positive variation and mental prosperity.

One vital part of strength is the capacity to successfully direct and deal with feelings. Feelings act as strong signs of inner states and assume a pivotal part in forming our reactions to stressors. People with high close to home strength can explore extraordinary feelings, like trepidation, bitterness, or outrage, without being overpowered by them. This close to home guideline adds to a more versatile reaction to testing circumstances, encouraging a feeling of control and strengthening.

Besides, mental cycles assume a vital part in flexibility. Mental adaptability, the ability to adjust thinking examples and viewpoints, permits people to reexamine difficulties and track down elective arrangements. Versatile people show a mental strength that empowers them to consider mishaps to be impermanent and conquerable, encouraging an uplifting perspective even notwithstanding misfortune. This mental reexamining adds to a versatile outlook that perspectives challenges as any open doors for development as opposed to impossible obstructions.

The job of social help in strength couldn't possibly be more significant. Solid relational associations and a dependable encouraging group of people contribute essentially to a singular's capacity to explore life's troubles.

Social help gives close to home approval, functional help, and a feeling of having a place, making a cradle against the pessimistic effect of stressors. Versatile people frequently draw strength from their informal organizations, whether it be family, companions, or local area, improving their ability to adjust to evolving conditions.

Flexibility, firmly connected to versatility, is the ability to change and flourish because of new circumstances. It includes an eagerness to embrace change, an adaptable mentality, and the capacity to gain from encounters. People with high versatility show an ability to change their way of behaving, perspectives, and objectives because of evolving conditions, cultivating a feeling of dominance and command over their lives.

The neurobiological premise of versatility and flexibility lies in the pliancy of the cerebrum. Brain adaptability alludes to the mind's capacity to redesign itself by shaping new brain associations. Encounters, both positive and negative, shape the mind's construction and capability, affecting how people answer pressure and misfortune. The cerebrum's versatility considers the advancement of strength through changes in brain processes that help survival strategies, profound guideline, and mental adaptability.

The investigation of antagonistic youth encounters (Pros) has given important bits of knowledge into the drawn out effect of early-life stressors on versatility. While openness to difficulty can present huge difficulties to psychological wellness, people with a background marked by Experts can foster strength through different instruments. Defensive elements, like positive connections, a strong climate, and admittance to assets, assume an essential part in moderating the impacts of early difficulty and encouraging strength.

The idea of post-horrendous development further investigates the extraordinary capability of affliction. Post-horrible development includes positive mental changes that people might encounter following a horrendous mishap. While injury can make inconvenient impacts, a few people rise up out of testing encounters with a recharged feeling of direction, expanded individual strength, and a more profound appreciation forever. This peculiarity highlights the limit with respect to strength and versatility to arise even in the consequence of critical difficulties.

With regards to transforming minds, which incorporates the consistent development of the human mind, flexibility and versatility become fundamental parts of mental prosperity. The steadily changing nature of the outside world, combined with inward changes in viewpoints, values, and life conditions, requires a unique way to deal with exploring the intricacies of the human experience.

Care rehearses, established in scrutinizing customs, offer mental devices for developing strength and flexibility in transforming minds. Care includes focusing on the current second with transparency and non-judgment.

By developing consciousness of contemplations, feelings, and sensations, people can foster a more grounded and focused way to deal with life's changes. Care rehearses, like contemplation and careful breathing, add to profound guideline, mental adaptability, and an expanded ability to adjust to new conditions.

The acknowledgment and responsibility treatment (ACT) system lines up with the standards of care and offers a mental procedure for building flexibility and versatility. ACT urges people to acknowledge their considerations and sentiments without judgment while resolving to activities lined up with their qualities. This approach cultivates mental adaptability, permitting people to adjust to changing conditions while remaining associated with their fundamental beliefs and objectives.

Positive brain science mediations give one more road to advancing flexibility and versatility in transforming minds. These intercessions center around developing positive feelings, qualities, and ethics to upgrade generally prosperity. Appreciation rehearses, like keeping an appreciation diary, have been connected to expanded life fulfillment and flexibility. By zeroing in on certain parts of life, people can foster a more hopeful standpoint, even despite progressing changes.

The idea of stream, presented by analyst Mihaly Csikszentmihalyi, lines up with the standards of flexibility in transforming minds. Stream alludes to a condition of ideal experience where people are completely submerged in a movement, forgetting about time and encountering a feeling of easy commitment. Embracing the stream state includes adjusting to the difficulties of the job needing to be done, keeping up with concentration, and tracking down characteristic fulfillment all the while. Stream encounters add to mental prosperity by upgrading versatility and flexibility notwithstanding powerful and developing conditions.

Individual account and the development of one's biography add to the improvement of flexibility and versatility in transforming minds. Account treatment, as evolved by Michael White and David Epston, stresses the job of stories in forming people's personalities and viewpoints. Investigating and rethinking individual accounts permits people to adjust their accounts in light of changing life conditions. This interaction cultivates a feeling of organization and creation, empowering people to explore the continuous development of their characters and encounters.

The idea of mental hold, established in neuroscience, gives experiences into the mental parts of strength and flexibility in transforming minds. Mental hold alludes to the cerebrum's capacity to streamline execution and adjust to changes by using elective brain organizations. Mental save is worked through participating in mentally animating exercises, long lasting learning, and keeping up with social associations. People with a high mental save show upgraded mental adaptability, empowering them to adjust to new data and encounters.

With regards to transforming minds, the convergence of innovation and brain science offers the two difficulties and amazing open doors for building versatility and flexibility. The quick speed of mechanical headways presents steady changes in how people associate with data, impart, and explore the advanced scene. Computerized strength, a term arising in the area of cyberpsychology, alludes to the capacity to explore the web-based world securely and adjust to the developing computerized climate.

Innovative apparatuses, for example, emotional wellness applications and computer generated reality intercessions, give amazing open doors to people to foster mental abilities that upgrade strength and versatility. Advanced care applications offer directed contemplation and stress-decrease works out, adding to profound guideline and mental adaptability. Augmented reality recreations can establish controlled conditions for openness treatment, assisting people with building versatility notwithstanding unambiguous feelings of trepidation or fears.

The idea of natural strength, acquired from ecological science, offers a figurative focal point for understanding flexibility and versatility in transforming minds. Biological flexibility alludes to the limit of an environment to assimilate unsettling influences, adjust to evolving conditions, and keep up with fundamental capabilities. Essentially, people with high mental versatility can retain the effect of life's difficulties, adjust to developing conditions, and keep a feeling of direction and prosperity.

Chapter 7

Mindful Practices for Reality Shaping

In the clamoring embroidery of present day presence, people end up caught in the multifaceted dance among discernment and reality. The human brain, a striking instrument fit for exploring the huge region of considerations, feelings, and encounters, assumes a crucial part in molding the focal point through which we view the world. As we navigate the maze of day to day existence, it becomes basic to develop careful practices that upgrade our mindfulness as well as engage us to shape our own world.

At the center of careful living untruths the significant acknowledgment that our considerations hold the possibility to form the texture of our reality. By digging into the domains of care, people set out on an extraordinary excursion that goes past the shallow layers of schedule. Care welcomes us to draw in with the current second completely, cultivating an elevated feeling of mindfulness and association with our general surroundings.

One central practice in the domain of care is contemplation. Established in old customs, contemplation fills in as a passage to the inward scenes of the brain. Through centered consideration and breath mindfulness, people can explore the maze of their viewpoints, seeing without connection. The standard act of contemplation not just quiets the violent waters of the psyche yet additionally sustains a space for thoughtfulness and self-revelation.

As we explore the intricacies of the cutting edge world, the specialty of careful breathing arises as a signal of quietness. In the surge of day to day existence, the breath fills in as an anchor, a suggestion to get back to the current second. Straightforward yet significant, cognizant breathing adjusts the mood of the body to the rhythm of the brain, making an agreeable ensemble that resounds with the quintessence of care.

Careful breathing stretches out past the bounds of formal reflection, consistently coordinating into the back and forth movement of ordinary exercises. Whether tasting some tea, strolling in nature, or participating in routine undertakings, the breath turns into a steady friend, meshing a string of mindfulness into the texture of every second.

In the dance among inward breath and exhalation, people track down a safe-haven of tranquility in the midst of the disorder of the outside world.

The development of care likewise includes fostering a sharp familiarity with the considerations that cross the scene of the psyche. The psyche, a perpetual generator of contemplations, frequently drives people into the domains of disappointments or future nerves. Careful mindfulness welcomes us to notice these psychological examples without judgment, cultivating a non-receptive position that frees us from the shackles of constant reasoning.

The act of care in thought perception discloses the ability to pick the contemplations that shape our existence deliberately. By perceiving the transient idea of considerations, people can segregate from pessimistic twistings and divert the concentration towards valuable and enabling mental scenes. This deliberate change in thought designs establishes the groundwork for a reality molded by energy and flexibility.

In the embroidery of careful living, the idea of temporariness arises as a central string. Recognizing the ephemeral idea of all things, including contemplations and feelings, frees people from the hold of connection and abhorrence. The consciousness of temporariness turns into a directing power, inciting people to enjoy the excellence of temporary minutes and explore difficulties with a feeling of serenity.

Care expands its arrive at past the singular domain, pervading the elements of relational connections. The act of careful correspondence turns into a foundation in cultivating association and understanding. By developing undivided attention and present-second mindfulness, people can participate in discussions with a profundity that rises above superficial communications.

Careful correspondence includes the words verbally expressed as well as the aim behind them. The specialty of talking with care requires a cognizant decision of language that is both valid and sympathetic. In the cauldron of careful correspondence, people manufacture bonds based on compassion and common regard, making a space for open exchange and mutual perspective.

As people leave on the excursion of reality forming through care, the investigation of mindfulness becomes the dominant focal point. The thoughtful look turns internal, disentangling layers of molded convictions and cultural builds. Through self-reflection, people gain understanding into the true center of their being, cultivating a significant arrangement between internal qualities and outward activities.

The scene of mindfulness reaches out to the domain of the capacity to appreciate people on a profound level, where people explore the rich embroidery of sentiments with care and sympathy. Instead of smothering or surrendering to feelings, care welcomes people to notice them with a non-critical mindfulness. This approach develops profound versatility, empowering people to answer life's difficulties with beauty and serenity.

In the domain of careful living, the idea of presence arises as a core value. Presence includes a profound commitment with the ongoing second, rising above the interruptions of the past and the vulnerabilities representing things to come. From the perspective of presence, people find the wealth of every second, opening the way to a reality that unfurls with clearness and reason.

The act of presence reaches out past individual prosperity, impacting the shared awareness of networks and social orders. Careful social orders are established in the standards of sympathy, compassion, and social obligation. The far reaching influence of individual care grows to make an aggregate mindfulness that rises above limits, cultivating a feeling of interconnectedness and shared mankind.

The reconciliation of care into the texture of cultural designs delivers a change in perspective in the manner people connect with the climate and the more extensive biological system. Careful stewardship of the planet arises as a characteristic expansion of the mindfulness developed through care rehearses. People become principled overseers of the Earth, perceiving the association between human prosperity and the soundness of the planet.

Chasing reality forming, the investigation of values and reason arises as an imperative compass. Care guides people to adjust their activities to values that resound with the center of their being. By living together as one with one's qualities, people manufacture a way that is genuine and reason driven, rising above cultural assumptions and outside approvals.

The excursion of reality molding through care envelops the coordination of psyche, body, and soul. Careful development rehearses, for example, yoga and judo, become conductors for epitomizing the standards of mindfulness and presence. Through the association of breath and development, people orchestrate the physical and mental aspects, cultivating a comprehensive prosperity that reaches out past the bounds of the mat.

Careful sustenance fills in as one more door to all encompassing prosperity, welcoming people to develop a cognizant relationship with food. The demonstration of careful eating includes enjoying each nibble with complete focus, recognizing the sustenance given by the Earth. In the careful utilization of food, people foster a significant association with the patterns of nature and the mind boggling snare of life that supports every one of us.

The far reaching material of reality forming through care unfurls in the domain of imagination and development. The development of a careful mentality supports a space for motivation to thrive. By calming the unremitting babble of the brain, people tap into the wellspring of imagination that lives in the profundities of cognizance. Careful inventiveness turns into a dance among instinct and articulation, birthing thoughts that have the ability to change the world.

As people cross the scene of careful living, the idea of care in real life comes first. Careful activity includes a cognizant and purposeful commitment with the jobs that needs to be done. Whether in the work environment, at home, or locally, people implant each activity with care, raising the nature of their commitments and encouraging a culture of greatness.

The reconciliation of care into the expert circle delivers a change in outlook in the manner in which people approach work. Careful initiative arises as a groundbreaking power that rises above customary orders. Pioneers directed by care typify character-istics of sympathy, versatility, and visionary reasoning, establishing a workplace that supports the development and prosperity of all colleagues.

Care in the work environment stretches out to the idea of careful navigation. By developing an uplifted consciousness of the basic inspirations and outcomes of choices, people explore the intricacies of decisions with lucidity and moral insight. Careful navigation turns into a compass that guides people and associations towards ways that line up with their qualities and long haul vision.

In the domain of training, the mixture of care rehearses turns into a foundation in sustaining the all encompassing improvement of understudies. Careful learning conditions focus on scholastic greatness as well as the prosperity and the capacity to understand anyone on a profound level of understudies. The combination of care into instructive educational plans outfits understudies with the devices to explore the difficulties of existence with versatility and a development mentality.

The excursion of reality molding through care stretches out to the domain of medical services, where careful practices are perceived for their remedial advantages. Careful ways to deal with wellbeing and prosperity include the treatment of side effects as well as the development of a comprehensive comprehension of the person. Care based mediations, for example, Care Based Pressure Decrease (MBSR), become necessary parts in advancing mental, close to home, and actual wellbeing.

In the embroidery of careful living, the idea of intergenerational care arises as a signal for what's in store. The transmission of care rehearses starting with one age then onto the next makes a tradition of insight and strength. By imparting the upsides of presence, sympathy, and cognizant residing in people in the future, people add to the co-making of an existence where care isn't simply a training however an approach to being.

The excursion of reality molding through care isn't without its difficulties. In a world that frequently commends performing multiple tasks and ceaseless hecticness, the development of care requires a cognizant responsibility and commitment. The interruptions of the computerized age, combined with the requests of a speedy society, present imposing snags on the way of careful living.

However, it is exactly even with these difficulties that the force of care sparkles splendidly. Care isn't a getaway from the real factors of life yet a route device that enables people to address difficulties with clearness and versatility. The act of care fills in as an anchor in the tempest, establishing people right now and giving a safe-haven of quietness in the midst of the tornado of outside pressures.

As people cross the scenes of their own personalities, developing care turns into a deep rooted excursion of self-revelation and development. The way of reality forming through care isn't an objective yet a nonstop unfurling, an investigation of the endless conceivable outcomes that live inside the current second. In the dance among mindfulness and activity, people become co-makers of their world, winding around an embroidery of presence that mirrors the magnificence of a careful and deliberate life.

All in all, careful practices for reality molding offer a significant greeting to people trying to explore the intricacies of the cutting edge world with clearness and reason. From the essential acts of reflection and careful breathing to the complex dance of careful correspondence and presence, the excursion of care unfurls as an extraordinary odyssey that reaches out into each feature of life.

The standards of care not just enable people to shape their own world yet in addition add to the aggregate development of society towards a more humane, cognizant, and interconnected presence.

As the strings of care wind through the embroidery of individual and shared mindset, another worldview of reality arises — one that is moored right now, lined up with legitimate qualities, and directed by the insight of care.

7.1 Introduce mindfulness and meditation as tools for mind morphing

In the multifaceted dance of presence, where the brain crosses the huge scenes of considerations, feelings, and encounters, the idea of care arises as a directing light — an extraordinary device that welcomes people to draw in with the current second in a significant and deliberate manner. At its pith, care is the craft of developing mindfulness, a perspective that includes focusing on the ongoing involvement in receptiveness, interest, and non-judgment.

Fundamental to the act of care is the thought that the brain holds the ability to shape one's view of the real world. By focusing on cognizant the current second, people gain knowledge into the routine examples of thought and feeling that frequently direct their reactions to the world. In this elevated condition of mindfulness, the psyche turns into a material whereupon people can deliberately paint the shades of their viewpoints, molding their mental scene with clearness and reason.

Reflection, a foundation of care, fills in as a strong vehicle for mind transforming. Established in old scrutinizing customs, contemplation is a training that includes purposefully centering the brain to accomplish an elevated condition of mindfulness, unwinding, and clearness. While there are different reflection strategies, the consistent idea among them is the development of a non-receptive and perceptive mentality.

One principal contemplation practice is breath mindfulness. By focusing on the breath — its beat, sensation, and stream — people make a mark of center that secures them right now. The musical breathe in and breathe out act as a passage to a condition of internal quietness, where the changes of the brain steadily settle, uncovering a space of serenity and clearness.

Careful contemplation stretches out past the demonstration of sitting in tranquility. It includes a powerful commitment with the brain's variances, permitting people to notice considerations and feelings without connection or repugnance. In the act of care contemplation, people become observers to the steadily changing scene of their inside world, making a space for self-revelation and psyche transforming.

The groundbreaking force of care and contemplation lies in their capacity to reshape the brain processes of the mind. Logical examination has enlightened the brain adaptability of the cerebrum, showing that the psyche has the exceptional ability to revamp itself in view of involvement and purposeful preparation. Care contemplation, with its accentuation on centered consideration and present-second mindfulness, has been displayed to actuate primary and utilitarian changes in the cerebrum that add to upgraded mental working and profound prosperity.

One vital region of the cerebrum that goes through massive changes through care practice is the prefrontal cortex. Frequently alluded to as the "President of the cerebrum," the prefrontal cortex assumes a vital part in leader works, for example, consideration, direction, and close to home guideline. Care reflection has been connected to an expansion in prefrontal cortex movement, prompting enhancements in mental control, close to home strength, and the capacity to keep up with center in the midst of interruptions.

Moreover, the amygdala, a locale related with the handling of feelings, shows changes because of care rehearses. Normal contemplation has been displayed to hose the amygdala's reactivity to stress and pessimistic upgrades, decreasing the power of profound reactions. This neurobiological shift adds to a more noteworthy close to home equilibrium and an expanded ability to explore testing circumstances with serenity.

The act of care and contemplation likewise impacts the default mode organization (DMN), an organization of interconnected cerebrum locales that becomes dynamic during times of psyche meandering and self-referential considerations. Care reflection is related with a diminishing in the movement of the DMN, prompting a decrease at the top of the priority list meandering and a more noteworthy capacity to remain present. This change in the default method of the cerebrum encourages a condition of careful mindfulness that reaches out past the conventional act of reflection into the texture of regular day to day existence.

Past the neurobiological changes, care and contemplation introduce a significant change in the manner people connect with their viewpoints and feelings. The noncritical mindfulness developed through these practices engages people to break liberated from the grasp of programmed responses and constant examples. Rather than being detainees of their own contemplations, people become cognizant planners of their psychological scene, deliberately picking considerations that line up with their qualities and goals.

In the domain of feeling guideline, care gives a safe-haven to people to investigate the rich embroidery of their sentiments with sympathy and composure. Instead of being cleared away by the flows of feelings, people foster the ability to notice close to home states without being overpowered. This shift from reactivity to responsiveness establishes the groundwork for the capacity to understand people on a deeper level — a vital part of psyche transforming.

Care and reflection likewise encourage an elevated identity mindfulness. As people take part in the act of turning internal, investigating the profundities of their viewpoints and feelings, they gain understanding into the molded examples of the psyche. This thoughtful excursion reveals the layers of character and conviction frameworks that frequently work underneath the outer layer of cognizant mindfulness, offering a chance for people to rethink and line up with their genuine selves.

The idea of care as a device for mind transforming reaches out past the singular domain to impact the elements of relational connections. Careful correspondence, established in the standards of presence and undivided attention, turns into a conductor for more profound association and understanding. The act of careful correspondence includes communicating one's thoughts with clearness and realness as well as adjusting to the verbal and non-verbal signs of others with compassion and veritable interest.

With regards to connections, care welcomes people to explore the intricacies of human association with an uplifted feeling of mindfulness. By pointing out careful the subtleties of collaborations, people encourage a space for common comprehension and empathy. The specialty of social care includes developing characteristics like tolerance, sympathy, and non-reactivity, establishing an agreeable climate that upholds the development and prosperity of the two people.

The standards of care additionally stretch out to the domain of direction. Careful direction includes a purposeful and cognizant way to deal with decisions, taking into account the quick results as well as the drawn out influence on one's prosperity and the prosperity of others. By carrying care to the dynamic interaction, people become sensitive to their qualities and needs, directing them towards decisions that resound with their valid selves.

The extraordinary excursion of brain transforming through care is reflected in the idea of care in real life. Careful activity includes injecting each part of existence with cognizant mindfulness, from routine errands to proficient undertakings. Whether in the work environment, at home, or locally, people approach activities with deliberateness and presence, making a gradually expanding influence that reaches out into the texture of their world.

Careful initiative arises as a characteristic result of psyche transforming through care. Pioneers who exemplify care standards are portrayed by characteristics like mindfulness, the capacity to understand individuals on a deeper level, and a dream that rises above quick difficulties. Careful pioneers move and engage everyone around them, establishing a workplace that encourages imagination, joint effort, and a feeling of direction.

With regards to training, care turns into an impetus for all encompassing turn of events. Careful learning conditions focus on scholastic greatness as well as the prosperity and the ability to appreciate anyone on a profound level of understudies. Incorporating care into instructive educational programs outfits understudies with significant devices for exploring the intricacies of life, advancing flexibility, center, and an empathetic comprehension of themselves as well as other people.

The utilization of care as a device for mind transforming is especially obvious in the domain of wellbeing and prosperity. Care based mediations, for example, Care Based Pressure Decrease (MBSR), have been embraced in medical services settings as compelling methodologies for

diminishing pressure, overseeing persistent torment, and working on generally speaking mental and actual wellbeing. The coordination of care into medical services perceives the indivisible association between the brain and the body, underscoring a comprehensive way to deal with prosperity.

As people leave on the excursion of psyche transforming through care, the idea of care in the public eye arises as a groundbreaking power. Careful social orders are portrayed by a shared perspective that values sympathy, compassion, and social obligation. The far reaching influence of individual care stretches out to make a cultural texture woven with strings of interconnectedness and shared mankind.

The act of care stretches out its compass to ecological stewardship, perceiving the interconnectedness between human prosperity and the strength of the planet. Careful living includes a cognizant familiarity with the effect of individual and aggregate activities on the climate. By developing a feeling of obligation towards the Earth, people add to the co-production of a supportable and amicable world.

7.2 Discuss the benefits of mindfulness in reducing stress and enhancing cognitive flexibility

Care, established in old thoughtful customs, has arisen as an amazing asset in contemporary brain science and health rehearses. Its applications stretch out a long ways past otherworldly or reflective domains, tracking down a critical spot in tending to the difficulties of present day life. One of the essential regions where care sparkles is in pressure decrease, cultivating a significant effect on mental prosperity. Additionally, its impact on mental adaptability adds one more layer of importance, improving the versatile limit of the psyche. In investigating the advantages of care in these spaces, it becomes obvious that its training offers a comprehensive way to deal with developing versatility and mental lucidity.

Stress, a ubiquitous power in the present speedy world, appears in different structures and forces. From working environment tensions to individual difficulties, people wrestle with stressors that can adversely influence both mental and actual wellbeing. Care, at its center, urges people to participate in the current second without judgment.

This purposeful mindfulness shapes the underpinning of pressure decrease methods related with care rehearses. By developing care, people foster the ability to notice their considerations and feelings without becoming entrapped in them.

The act of care contemplation fills in as a foundation in pressure decrease endeavors. This type of contemplation includes focusing on the breath, sensations in the body, or a point of convergence, consequently diverting the brain from pressure prompting considerations. Logical examinations have reliably exhibited the viability of care contemplation in decreasing feelings of anxiety. The physiological changes related with care, for example, diminished cortisol levels and further developed pulse changeability, add to a stronger pressure reaction.

Care Based Pressure Decrease (MBSR), created by Dr. Jon Kabat-Zinn, represents the organized incorporation of care into a program explicitly intended for pressure decrease. MBSR integrates different care works on, including reflection and careful development, offering members an exhaustive tool compartment to oversee pressure. Research concentrates on MBSR have revealed critical decreases in pressure related side effects, going from tension to persistent agony. The development of care, as confirmed by these projects, arises as a strong counteractant to the inescapable impact of pressure.

Past the prompt decrease of pressure, care causes a change in context that encourages long haul strength. By fostering an attention to the temporariness of contemplations and feelings, people become less inclined to being overpowered by the difficulties they face. Care energizes the acknowledgment that pressure is a transient encounter, and one can pick how to answer it. This shift from receptive to responsive conduct underlies the groundbreaking force of care in overseeing pressure.

Mental adaptability, a pivotal mental expertise, alludes to the capacity to adjust one's reasoning in light of evolving conditions. It includes receptiveness to new data, the capacity to move points of view, and the ability to engage various perspectives. With regards to care, the development of mental adaptability happens naturally through the act of non-critical mindfulness. As people become more sensitive to their viewpoints and feelings, they foster a psychological nimbleness that takes into consideration versatile reactions to testing circumstances.

Care rehearses, especially those stressing open mindfulness, add to the upgrade of mental adaptability. At the point when people take part in care reflection, they figure out how to notice their contemplations without connection or repugnance. This interaction encourages a non-responsive mindfulness that is primary to mental adaptability. Rather than inflexibly will undoubtedly assumptions or ongoing idea designs, people rehearsing care become more open to elective viewpoints and arrangements.

Neuroscientific research gives important experiences into the components through which care impacts mental adaptability. Useful attractive reverberation imaging (fMRI) studies have shown changes in cerebrum areas related with consideration and mental control following care preparing. The prefrontal cortex, a key region engaged with leader capabilities, displays expanded movement in people who routinely practice care. These neurobiological changes line up with the noticed enhancements in mental adaptability announced in care research.

Additionally, care mediations have shown viability in clinical populaces where mental adaptability deficiencies are common. For example, people with uneasiness issues or melancholy frequently show inflexible reasoning examples that add to the ingenuity of their side effects.

Care based mediations, for example, Care Based Mental Treatment (MBCT), focus on these mental rigidities by coordinating care rehearses with mental conduct treatment standards. The cooperative energy among care and mental treatment demonstrates viable in forestalling the repeat of burdensome episodes and advancing mental adaptability.

The entwining advantages of care in pressure decrease and mental adaptability make a positive criticism circle. As stress reduces through care rehearses, mental assets recently involved by pressure related considerations become accessible for additional versatile mental cycles. This redistribution of mental assets adds to an improved limit with regards to adaptable reasoning and critical thinking. Basically, the development of care fills in as an impetus for a positive outpouring of mental prosperity.

The effects of care on pressure and mental adaptability stretch out past the singular level, affecting relational elements and hierarchical societies. In work environment settings, where stress is much of the time an unavoidable power, care programs have built up some momentum as a technique for advancing representative prosperity and hierarchical viability. Careful initiative, described by pioneers who exemplify and advance care rehearses, establishes the vibe for a workplace that values presence, cooperation, and flexibility.

Associations that coordinate care into their corporate culture report upgrades in worker fulfillment, decreased burnout rates, and improved imagination. Care based mediations in the work environment frequently incorporate instructional meetings that show representatives how to apply care standards amidst their expert obligations. By cultivating an aggregate mindfulness and strength, associations can explore difficulties all the more really and make a culture that focuses on the prosperity of its individuals.

The instruction area additionally stands to profit from the reconciliation of care rehearses. Understudies, confronting scholastic tensions and the requests of a quickly impacting world, can foster fundamental adapting abilities through care training. Projects, for example, Careful Schools have arisen to present care rehearses in instructive settings, giving understudies and educators devices to oversee pressure and improve mental abilities.

In the domain of medical care, care based mediations have shown guarantee in tending to different circumstances, from constant agony to sleep deprivation. Care Based Pressure Decrease (MBSR) programs have been incorporated into clinical settings, offering patients an integral way to deal with conventional clinical medicines. The brain body association stressed in care rehearses lines up with an all encompassing way to deal with medical services, recognizing the exchange among mental and actual prosperity.

The use of care in clinical brain science has extended to envelop a scope of remedial modalities. Care Based Mental Treatment (MBCT), Rationalistic Conduct Treatment (DBT), and Acknowledgment and Responsibility Treatment (ACT) are instances of helpful methodologies that integrate care standards. These treatments plan to improve mental adaptability, lessen side effect seriousness, and forestall the repeat of emotional well-being difficulties.

The advantages of care in pressure decrease and mental adaptability are not restricted to grown-ups; they reach out to youngsters and youths. Care programs in schools affect understudies' close to home guideline, attentional control, and inter-active abilities. By furnishing youthful personalities with care instruments, instructors add to the improvement of strong people fit for exploring the intricacies of their own and scholarly lives.

As care earns respect for its positive effect on psychological well-being and pros-perity, scientists keep on investigating the fundamental components and expected applications. The field of scrutinizing neuroscience examines how care rehearses shape the construction and capability of the cerebrum. Concentrates on utilizing progressed neuroimaging procedures, like dissemination tensor imaging (DTI) and electro-encephalography (EEG), give important bits of knowledge into the brain changes related with care.

One striking area of exploration is the assessment of the default mode organization (DMN), an organization of mind districts dynamic during rest and self-referential reasoning. Care rehearses have been found to balance the action and network inside the DMN, proposing a connection among care and the guideline of self-referential perspectives. This brain regulation lines up with the noticed decreases in rumination and overthinking, adding to the pressure lessening impacts of care.

Moreover, studies investigating the brain adaptability of the cerebrum uncover that care can actuate primary changes in districts related with close to home guideline and mental control. The hippocampus, associated with memory and learning, and the amygdala, fundamental to the handling of feelings, show changes in volume and net-work following care mediations. These neurobiological changes give a neuroscientific establishment to the noticed upgrades in pressure strength and mental adaptability related with care rehearses.

The likely utilizations of care stretch out to the domain of innovation, where cre-ative arrangements influence care standards to advance prosperity. Care applications, computer generated reality encounters, and biofeedback gadgets offer people open apparatuses for integrating care into their regular routines. While these innovations can't completely reproduce the profundity of a customary care practice, they give a door to people to investigate and coordinate care into their schedules.

In spite of the developing collection of proof supporting the advantages of care, difficulties and misguided judgments continue. Wariness might emerge from an impression of care as a panacea or a stylish self improvement instrument without logical establishing. It is fundamental to explain that care is definitely not a one-size-fits-all arrangement; rather, an expertise requires practice and variation to individual necessities and inclinations.

Also, care isn't inseparable from inactivity or the shortfall of testing feelings. Care welcomes people to confront their encounters with an open and non-critical mindfulness, which might incorporate recognizing and managing inconvenience. The confusion that care is tied in with exhausting the psyche or accomplishing a consistent condition of quiet neglects its nuanced nature and the wealth of the current second, which envelops a range of feelings and encounters.

Social assignment and the secularization of care present moral contemplations that warrant consideration. Care begins from Buddhist insightful customs, and its extraction from its social and otherworldly setting can prompt the distortion of its standards. Careful mindfulness, as grasped in its conventional roots, envelops a significant moral structure and an extraordinary excursion that stretches out past pressure decrease and mental upgrade. Care professionals and teachers bear the obligation of safeguarding the respectability of care while adjusting its applications to assorted social and mainstream settings.

In addition, the commodification of care in the wellbeing business brings up issues about its openness and inclusivity. Care, frequently bundled as an attractive item, may become distant to the individuals who can't manage the cost of costly retreats or premium care applications. Guaranteeing that care stays a device for the aggregate prosperity of society requires resolving issues of openness and advancing comprehensive methodologies that oblige different financial foundations.

All in all, the advantages of care in diminishing pressure and improving mental adaptability are complex and stretch out across individual, relational, and cultural levels. The act of care, established in old insight and upheld by contemporary examination, offers a groundbreaking way to deal with exploring the intricacies of present day life. From stress decrease procedures to the development of mental adaptability, care enables people to draw in with their encounters such that cultivates prosperity and flexibility.

As care keeps on incorporating into different spaces, including medical services, instruction, and the working environment, its capability to add to a more humane and versatile society turns out to be progressively clear. The cooperative energy between old insightful customs and current logical request gives a powerful establishment to understanding and outfitting the advantages of care. Embracing care as an expertise to be developed, as opposed to a temporary pattern, holds the way to opening its maximum capacity in advancing psychological well-being, versatility, and a more profound association with the current second.

7.3 Provide guided exercises for incorporating mindfulness into daily life

Integrating care into day to day existence requires goal, practice, and a pledge to developing mindfulness amidst different exercises. Care isn't restricted to formal reflection meetings; it is an approach to being that can be coordinated into the texture of ordinary encounters. The accompanying directed practices offer commonsense strategies for mixing care into various parts of day to day existence, encouraging a more profound association with the current second and advancing in general prosperity.

Careful Breathing In the midst of Routine Exercises:

Start by pointing out your breath during routine exercises, like washing dishes or strolling. Center around the vibe of the breath entering and leaving the body. Notice the ascent and fall of your chest or the extension and constriction of your midsection. Permit the breath to be an anchor, establishing you right now. In the event that your psyche meanders, delicately guide it back to the breath. This straightforward practice can transform unremarkable exercises into open doors for care.

Careful Eating:

Change the demonstration of eating into a careful encounter. Begin by noticing the varieties, surfaces, and scents of your food. Pause for a minute to offer thanks for the sustenance it gives. Bite gradually and appreciate each chomp, focusing on the flavors and sensations in your mouth. Be completely present with the demonstration of eating, forgoing interruptions like sitting in front of the television or looking at your telephone. This training improves the satisfaction in feasts as well as advances a more prominent familiarity with yearning and completion signs.

Body Output Contemplation:

Put away opportunity for a body filter contemplation, either toward the beginning of the day or before sleep time. Track down an agreeable position, either sitting or resting, and carry attention to various pieces of your body, beginning from your toes and bit by bit climbing to the highest point of your head. Notice any sensations, strain, or areas of unwinding. Assuming you experience strain, inhale into that area and picture the pressure delivering with each breathe out. This training advances body mindfulness and unwinding.

Careful Strolling:

Transform your everyday stroll into a care practice. As you walk, focus on the impression of your feet connecting with the ground. Feel the mood of your means and the development of your body. Notice the sights and sounds around you — the stirring of leaves, the peeping of birds. Assuming your psyche begins to meander, delicately take it back to the experience of strolling. This strolling reflection can bring a feeling of quiet and presence to your day to day work-out daily schedule.

Careful Correspondence:

Carry care into your connections with others. At the point when taken part in a discussion, practice undivided attention by completely zeroing in on the speaker without figuring out your reaction in your brain. Notice their manner of speaking, their non-verbal communication, and the feelings behind their words. Know about your own responses and reactions. This careful correspondence cultivates a more profound association and figuring out in your connections.

Careful Innovation Use:

In a world immersed with innovation, rehearsing care in your computerized cooperations is fundamental. Prior to going after your telephone or PC, pause for a minute to focus yourself. Be aware of the expectation behind your innovation use. Whether it's answering messages, looking at web-based entertainment, or watching recordings, move toward every action with care. Set explicit times for tech breaks and use them purposefully, keeping away from thoughtless looking over.

Careful Work Breaks:

Integrate care into your business day by enjoying careful reprieves. Move back from your work area and track down a calm space. Shut your eyes and take a couple of full breaths. Carry your attention to the current second, permitting considerations about work to briefly blur. Take part in a concise body filter, checking in with any areas of pressure. This careful break can invigorate your psyche and improve your center when you return to work.

Careful Appreciation Journaling:

Make an everyday appreciation journaling practice. Toward the start or end of every day, record three things you are thankful for. These can be straightforward or significant, zeroing in on both the delights and difficulties. As you think about every thing, enjoy the sensations of appreciation. This training develops a positive outlook and improves consciousness of the positive parts of your life.

Careful Night Reflection:

Prior to sleep time, take part in a careful reflection on your day. Take a couple of seconds to survey the occasions, cooperations, and feelings of the day. Without judgment, notice any snapshots of euphoria, stress, or learning. Consider how you answered difficulties and express self-sympathy for any challenges. This intelligent practice assists you with incorporating care into your everyday encounters and readies your brain for a relaxing rest.

Cherishing Thoughtfulness Reflection:

Devote time to a cherishing thoughtfulness reflection, stretching out generosity and sympathy to yourself as well as other people. Track down an agreeable position, shut your eyes, and spotlight on sending positive goals.

Start by coordinating these sentiments towards yourself, then, at that point, bit by bit extend to incorporate friends and family, colleagues, and, surprisingly, those with whom you might have difficulties. This training encourages a feeling of association and sympathy, advancing a good and kind way to deal with life.

Integrating care into day to day existence is a continuous cycle that advances with reliable practice. Explore different avenues regarding these directed activities, adjusting them to suit your inclinations and timetable. The pith of care lies in carrying non-critical attention to every second, encouraging a more profound comprehension of yourself and your general surroundings. As you coordinate these practices into your everyday daily schedule, you might find an elevated feeling of presence, strength, and generally prosperity.

Chapter 8

Ethical Considerations in Reality Shaping

Moral contemplations truly molding include a mind boggling and complex scene that converges with different spaces, going from innovation and man-made brainpower to brain research and theory. As mankind keeps on pushing the limits of development, the requirement for an insightful and complete assessment of the moral ramifications of reality molding turns out to be progressively principal.

At the core of moral contemplations actually molding lies the crossing point of force, control, and obligation. The actual thought of molding reality suggests a specific degree of impact over the world and the people inside it. Whether it be through trend setting innovations, social frameworks, or mental intercessions, the moral elements of such impact request cautious investigation.

One of the essential regions where reality molding brings moral worries is up in the turn of events and arrangement of arising advancements. Man-made brainpower (artificial intelligence), for example, can possibly reshape how we live, work, and associate with the world. From independent vehicles to algorithmic direction, the moral ramifications of these advancements are huge and changed.

One vital moral thought in man-made intelligence is the issue of predisposition. Man-made intelligence frameworks are just however fair as the information on which they seem to be prepared. Assuming that the preparation information is one-sided, the simulated intelligence framework can propagate and try and worsen existing social imbalances. This brings up issues about decency, equity, and the potential for innovation to either support or challenge cultural standards.

Besides, the utilization of artificial intelligence in reconnaissance and security attack is a developing concern. As state run administrations and organizations convey modern observation innovations, people's all in all correct to protection is progressively compromised. The moral issue lies in tracking down a harmony between the possible advantages of upgraded security and the assurance of individual opportunities.

One more part of reality molding that requests moral examination is the domain of virtual and increased reality. These innovations can possibly make vivid and extraordinary encounters, obscuring the lines between the physical and virtual universes. As clients explore these other real factors, questions emerge about assent, validness, and the potential for control.

Consider a situation where people can change their view of reality through virtual encounters. While this might offer restorative advantages, it additionally brings up moral issues about the outcomes of disengaging from this present reality. What are the ramifications for psychological wellness, social connections, and our comprehension of true reality?

In the domain of virtual entertainment and online stages, reality molding takes on an alternate structure. The calculations that curate our internet based encounters have the ability to shape our insights, impact our choices, and even add to the polarization of society. The moral obligation of tech organizations in planning and carrying out these calculations is a basic thought.

Issues, for example, falsehood, protected, closed off environments, and the spread of fanatic belief systems feature the moral difficulties of reality molding in the computerized age. The control of popular assessment through designated content and algorithmic suggestions highlights the requirement for a proactive and moral way to deal with content balance and stage administration.

Past the mechanical space, moral contemplations in actuality molding stretch out to the area of brain research. The investigation of human way of behaving and perception gives experiences into how people see and develop their real factors. Analysts and conduct researchers wrestle with the moral ramifications of intercessions that mean to profoundly impact conduct and discernment.

For example, the utilization of social prods in open approach brings up issues about the independence and educated assent regarding people. While bumps can energize positive ways of behaving, for example, better way of life decisions, the moral limit among impact and control becomes obscured. Understanding the subtleties of human direction is critical in exploring the moral scene of reality forming in brain research.

The idea of informed assent turns out to be especially remarkable while investigating the crossing point of reality molding and neurotechnology. Progresses in neuroscience raise the chance of straightforwardly communicating with the human mind to improve mental capacities or treat neurological problems. Notwithstanding, the moral ramifications of such mediations, particularly without any completely educated assent, require cautious thought.

Besides, the potential for neuromarketing to impact buyer conduct presents moral difficulties. On the off chance that organizations can use neuroscientific bits of knowledge to control shopper inclinations at an inner mind level, questions emerge about the limits of moral promoting rehearses and the insurance of individual independence.

Thoughtfully, the investigation of reality forming dives into inquiries concerning the idea of reality itself. As people and social orders apply expanding command over their surroundings, the well established philosophical investigation into the idea of truth and presence takes on new aspects. Moral contemplations here reach out to the actual underpinnings of how we might interpret reality and the ramifications of reshaping it.

The moral talk on reality molding isn't restricted to the possible dangers and entanglements yet additionally incorporates the valuable open doors and obligations that accompany the ability to shape the world. In imagining a positive and morally grounded way to deal with reality molding, cooperation among different partners becomes basic.

A critical part of moral reality molding is inclusivity and guaranteeing that the advantages are conveyed impartially. As new innovations and mediations arise, there is a gamble of intensifying existing imbalances. The moral basic is to effectively address these abberations and guarantee that the advantages of reality forming are open to all citizenry.

Straightforwardness and responsibility are basic mainstays of moral reality forming. Whether in the advancement of man-made intelligence calculations, the sending of computer generated reality encounters, or the execution of social mediations, straightforwardness cultivates trust and

permits people to go with informed choices. Moral rules and guidelines should be laid out and complied with across enterprises to guarantee capable and responsible reality molding rehearses.

Instructive drives assume a significant part in cultivating moral mindfulness and capability as a general rule forming. Since early on, people ought to be outfitted with the decisive reasoning abilities important to explore the intricacies of a world molded by innovation, brain research, and reasoning. Moral proficiency turns into a fundamental part of schooling in planning people to draw in with the moral components of reality forming.

Moreover, interdisciplinary coordinated effort is fundamental in tending to the diverse idea of moral reality molding. Uniting specialists from fields like innovation, brain research, reasoning, morals, regulation, and humanism takes into consideration an all encompassing comprehension of the difficulties and valuable open doors within reach. Cross-disciplinary exchange can prompt the advancement of extensive structures that guide moral dynamic in the unique scene of reality molding.

All in all, moral contemplations in actuality molding are at the front line of the cultural and mechanical headways of the 21st hundred years. The ability to shape reality accompanies significant obligations, requiring a smart and moral methodology across different spaces. Whether in the improvement of state of the art advancements, the investigation of virtual and expanded real factors, or the investigation of human way of behaving, the moral basic is to explore the intricacies of reality molding with care, straightforwardness, and a promise to the benefit of all. As we stand at the intersection of uncommon advancement, the decisions today will shape the real factors of tomorrow, and the moral contemplations that guide those decisions will characterize the future we by and large possess.

8.1 Explore the ethical implications of influencing personal and collective realities

Investigating the moral ramifications of impacting individual and aggregate real factors digs into a domain where the limits between individual independence, cultural prosperity, and innovative capacities meet. In a period described by fast progressions in innovation, correspondence, and social elements, the ability to shape individual and aggregate real factors has never been more articulated. This investigation unfurls across different aspects, going from the singular's all in all correct to self-assurance to the more extensive cultural effect of compelling powers forming shared accounts.

At the core of the moral talk lies the strain between individual independence and outside impact. Each individual has an essential right to shape their own existence, pursue decisions that line up with their qualities, and develop a story that mirrors their special personality.

Nonetheless, the coming of refined innovations, convincing correspondence techniques, and algorithmic direction presents an intricate interaction of impacts that might possibly think twice about independence.

Mechanical headways, especially in the fields of computerized reasoning and information examination, give devices to understanding and anticipating individual inclinations, ways of behaving, and dynamic examples. While these abilities offer extraordinary open doors for personalization and custom fitted encounters, they likewise raise moral worries about the limits of impact. The moral basic is to find some kind of harmony among customization and the safeguarding of individual organization.

In the domain of customized advances, for example, suggestion calculations, the moral contemplations become apparent. Calculations that curate content, propose items, or suggest social associations in view of client information can possibly make channel air pockets and protected, closed off environments. While the expectation may be to improve client experience, the potentially negative result is the support of existing convictions and viewpoints, restricting openness to assorted assessments and testing thoughts.

In addition, the moral ramifications of customized advances reach out to issues of protection and informed assent. Clients frequently exchange individual information for the accommodation and personalization presented by computerized stages. Be that as it may, the degree to which people know about and agree to the assortment and utilization of their information stays a quarrelsome issue. Straightforwardness in information rehearses, client control, and powerful information security guidelines become urgent in maintaining moral norms in the domain of customized advancements.

The impact on private real factors likewise reaches out to the field of virtual entertainment, where stages assume a huge part in forming general assessment, social standards, and individual discernments. The moral contemplations here rotate around the obligation of virtual entertainment organizations in directing substance, forestalling the spread of deception, and cultivating a solid web-based climate.

The plan decisions made by virtual entertainment stages, for example, the calculations that focus on happy, influence the data clients are presented to. The potential for these calculations to coincidentally add to the polarization of society or enhance hurtful stories requires an insightful assessment of the moral aspects. Finding some kind of harmony between opportunity of articulation and forestalling hurt turns into a focal test in guaranteeing moral impact on private and aggregate real factors through virtual entertainment.

Past the advanced domain, the moral ramifications of impacting individual real factors manifest in regions like showcasing and publicizing. The utilization of mental strategies to shape purchaser conduct brings up issues about the limits of moral influence.

Advertisers utilizing systems informed by social brain research, neuro-showcasing, or close to home control explore a scarce difference between morally advancing items and possibly taking advantage of weaknesses.

For instance, the moral utilization of powerful procedures in promoting would include straightforward correspondence, keeping away from misdirection, and regarding the independence of shoppers. The test lies in recognizing moral influence, which illuminates and enables people to go with informed decisions, and manipulative strategies that exploit mental predispositions or make counterfeit requirements.

With regards to aggregate real factors, the moral contemplations become significantly more multifaceted. Affecting cultural stories, social qualities, and shared convictions conveys huge ramifications for the prosperity of networks and the working of vote based systems. Media, both conventional and computerized, assumes a critical part in forming aggregate real factors, bringing up moral issues about editorial trustworthiness, publication obligation, and the scattering of data.

The peculiarity of "counterfeit news" and deception features the moral difficulties in the media scene. The intentional spread of bogus or deluding data can have significant outcomes on open discernment, political talk, and social attachment. The obligation of news sources to check data, maintain editorial norms, and focus on the public interest becomes principal in exploring the moral elements of affecting aggregate real factors.

Political impact, promulgation, and the control of popular assessment are longstanding moral worries that have taken on new aspects in the computerized age. The utilization of virtual entertainment stages for political informing, designated publicizing, and the spread of troublesome stories brings up issues about the moral limits of political correspondence. The potential for unfamiliar obstruction, algorithmic enhancement of fanatic perspectives, and the disintegration of confidence in fair establishments highlight the earnestness of tending to these moral difficulties.

The crossing point of innovation and a majority rules government presents novel moral contemplations, for example, the effect of algorithmic dynamic on discretionary cycles. The utilization of calculations to target and influence citizens, miniature focusing on in view of individual information, and the control of online talk during races bring up issues about the respectability of majority rule frameworks. Moral protections, straightforwardness in political publicizing, and the guideline of advanced battling become fundamental in safeguarding the vote based standards of decency and responsibility.

Notwithstanding political impact, the moral ramifications of affecting aggregate real factors reach out to issues of social portrayal and inclusivity. The accounts advanced in media, publicizing, and mainstream society add to the development of cultural standards and values.

Moral contemplations emerge when certain gatherings or viewpoints are minimized or distorted, supporting generalizations and propagating disparities.

Social apportionment, generalizing, and the commodification of assorted personalities in media and advertising are moral worries that request cautious examination. The obligation to depict different voices genuinely, challenge generalizations, and add to a more comprehensive and impartial portrayal turns into an ethical basic for content makers and powerhouses.

On a worldwide scale, the moral components of impacting aggregate real factors arise with regards to global relations and social trade. The power elements intrinsic in molding worldwide stories, discernments, and mentalities require moral contemplations to keep away from social government, neocolonialism, or the burden of predominant philosophies on assorted social orders.

As innovative capacities keep on advancing, the moral talk on affecting individual and aggregate real factors reaches out to arising areas like virtual and increased reality. These vivid innovations can possibly reshape how people see and communicate with the world, acquainting new moral difficulties related with assent, genuineness, and the obscuring of virtual and actual real factors.

Consider the moral ramifications of establishing virtual conditions that recreate certifiable encounters or change tangible discernments. The potential for augmented reality to be utilized for restorative purposes, schooling, or diversion brings up issues about the mental effect, expected habit, and the moral utilization of such incredible assets. Finding some kind of harmony between the advantages of vivid advances and the likely dangers to psychological well-being and prosperity turns into a focal worry in the moral investigation of virtual and expanded reality.

In exploring the moral ramifications of impacting individual and aggregate real factors, a basic rule is the acknowledgment of human nobility and the inborn worth of individual and aggregate organization. Maintaining basic freedoms, cultivating inclusivity, and regarding social variety ought to be at the cutting edge of moral contemplations in the plan, organization, and effect appraisal of advancements and correspondence techniques.

Instructive drives assume a urgent part in advancing moral mindfulness and capability in exploring the intricacies of impacting individual and aggregate real factors. From computerized education projects to media proficiency educational plans, people need the apparatuses to fundamentally assess data, figure out the moral elements of innovation, and go with informed decisions in the advanced scene.

Besides, interdisciplinary cooperation is fundamental in tending to the multilayered nature of moral impact. Uniting specialists from fields like innovation, morals, brain science, humanism, regulation, and correspondence takes into consideration a comprehensive comprehension of the difficulties and open doors within reach. Cross-disciplinary discourse can prompt the advancement of complete systems that guide moral dynamic in the unique scene of affecting individual and aggregate real factors.

8.2 Discuss the responsibility that comes with the power of shaping minds

The force of significantly shaping personalities is a powerful power that penetrates different parts of society, incorporating schooling, media, innovation, and social accounts. The significant effect of this power raises moral contemplations and requires a conversation on the obligation that goes with it. As people and organizations use the capacity to profoundly mold minds, they expect an honest conviction to do so morally, straightforwardly, and with a promise to encouraging positive results for people and society in general.

In the domain of training, the obligation of shaping personalities is especially apparent. Instructors, from educators in grade schools to teachers in advanced education, assume an essential part in forming the erudite person, close to home, and moral improvement of understudies. The substance they present, the qualities they ingrain, and the systems they utilize add to the arrangement of people's perspectives, decisive reasoning abilities, and moral compass.

Moral contemplations in training rotate around the standards of decency, inclusivity, and the advancement of balanced, informed residents. The substance picked for educational plans, the viewpoints introduced in homerooms, and the techniques for appraisal all impact how understudies see the world and their place in it. Instructors bear the obligation of giving a fair and various schooling that furnishes understudies with the devices to think basically, draw in with various perspectives, and settle on informed choices.

Besides, the ability to mold minds stretches out to the plan and execution of instructive innovations. As advanced instruments become vital to present day instruction, designers, and policymakers should think about the moral ramifications of these innovations. Issues like information security, algorithmic predispositions, and the advanced separation require cautious consideration regarding guarantee that instructive innovations contribute emphatically to the opportunity for growth without worsening existing disparities or undermining people's protection.

With regards to media, the obligation of shaping personalities is apparent in the accounts introduced through different channels, including media sources, amusement stages, and web-based entertainment. Media impacts general assessment, shapes social standards, and adds to the development of cultural accounts.

Writers, content makers, and media associations bear the moral obligation of giving exact data, keeping away from emotionalism, and cultivating a different and comprehensive portrayal of alternate points of view.

The ascent of online entertainment acquaints new aspects with the force of deeply shaping personalities. Calculations that curate content in view of client inclinations can make protected, closed off environments, where people are presented principally to data that lines up with their current convictions. This raises moral worries about the potential for deception, the polarization of society, and the effect on equitable talk. Web-based entertainment stages have an obligation to address these worries through straightforward calculations, hearty substance balance, and endeavors to relieve the spread of bogus data.

In the domain of publicizing and advertising, the ability to mold minds is saddled to impact customer conduct. Notices utilize different mental strategies to make want, advance items, and shape social standards. Moral contemplations emerge while advertising systems exploit weaknesses, propagate unsafe generalizations, or add to over the top commercialization. Mindful publicizing involves straightforwardness, legitimacy, and a guarantee to moral practices that focus on shopper prosperity.

Media outlets, including film, TV, and gaming, additionally holds the ability to profoundly mold minds by affecting social qualities and standards. Content makers, journalists, and makers have an obligation to think about the expected effect of their work on cultural perspectives. Moral narrating includes advancing variety, testing generalizations, and resolving social issues with responsiveness and subtlety. The obligation to impact minds through diversion stretches out to the depiction of emotional well-being, connections, and different viewpoints that add to cultural insights.

The coming of trend setting innovations, like man-made reasoning (computer based intelligence) and AI, presents new moral contemplations in the force of shaping personalities. Man-made intelligence calculations that suggest content, customize client encounters, or pursue choices in view of information can unintentionally sustain predispositions present in the preparation information. Designers and specialists bear the obligation of tending to these predispositions, guaranteeing straightforwardness in algorithmic direction, and relieving the expected adverse consequences on people and society.

The obligation of significantly shaping personalities additionally stretches out to social accounts that impact aggregate characters and cultural qualities. Scholars, specialists, and social powerhouses add to the development of stories that shape how networks see themselves as well as other people. Moral narrating includes perceiving the variety of encounters, keeping away from social appointment, and cultivating a feeling of incorporation that celebrates various voices and viewpoints.

In the domain of legislative issues, the ability to deeply impact minds is used through political correspondence, public talk, and the stories introduced by political pioneers. The moral obligation here lies in advancing honest and straightforward correspondence, keeping away from the control of popular assessment, and maintaining majority rule values. Political pioneers have an obligation to take part in dependable way of talking that cultivates solidarity, addresses cultural difficulties, and regards the standards of equity and basic liberties.

Strict and otherworldly pioneers additionally hold the ability to mold minds through the dispersal of moral and moral lessons. The obligation in this setting includes elevating values that add to the prosperity of people and society, cultivating resistance and understanding, and keeping away from the abuse of strict or profound expert for destructive purposes.

The convergence of innovation and medical services presents moral contemplations in the ability to impact minds through clinical mediations, like neuroenhancement and psychopharmacology. The improvement of mental upgrading drugs, mind machine interfaces, and different advancements that impact mental capability brings up issues about independence, assent, and the possible cultural ramifications of far reaching mental upgrade. Moral rules should address the capable utilization of these innovations to guarantee that they add to prosperity without compromising principal values.

The obligation of shaping personalities isn't restricted to explicit callings or areas; an aggregate commitment envelops all people who add to the development of thoughts, stories, and social standards. Moral contemplations in profoundly shaping personalities rotate around standards like regard for independence, advancement of prosperity, variety and consideration, straightforwardness, and a guarantee to honesty.

Instructive organizations assume an essential part in imparting moral qualities and decisive reasoning abilities that engage people to explore the intricacies of the data age. Media associations should stick to editorial morals, advancing exact and unprejudiced revealing. Content makers in different fields, from amusement to promoting, should think about the likely effect of their work on assorted crowds and cultural perspectives.

In the time of data and network, encouraging media education becomes basic to furnish people with the abilities to observe dependable data from falsehood, fundamentally assess content, and draw in with different points of view. Instructive projects and public mindfulness crusades assume a part in advancing media proficiency and enabling people to be knowing buyers of data.

Legitimate and administrative structures likewise add to significantly shaping personalities capably. Security regulations, purchaser assurance guidelines, and rules for content balance on advanced stages assist with laying out limits and moral norms.

Policymakers have an obligation to address the moral ramifications of arising innovations, guaranteeing that guidelines stay up with mechanical headways to safeguard people and society.

The moral obligation of shaping personalities requires continuous reflection, discourse, and variation to the developing difficulties introduced by mechanical, social, and social changes. It includes a promise to constant learning, receptiveness to different viewpoints, and an acknowledgment of the possible effect of one's activities on people and society.

All in all, the ability to mold minds accompanies a significant obligation to do so morally, straightforwardly, and with a promise to positive results for people and society. Whether in training, media, innovation, or social stories, the decisions made by people and establishments in shaping personalities add to the shared mindset of mankind. The moral basic is to cultivate a culture of dependable impact that focuses on independence, prosperity, inclusivity, and a promise to honesty and equity. As we explore the intricacies of a quickly impacting world, the obligation to deeply mold minds turns into an ethical compass directing our decisions in developing the stories, thoughts, and values that shape the future we all in all possess.

8.3 Analyze the potential for positive and negative consequences in reality morphing

Reality transforming, an idea including the change or change of seen reality, presents a scene ready with both potential for positive and unfortunate results. As mechanical progressions, mental experiences, and cultural movements merge, the ramifications of reality transforming stretch out across different areas, including innovation, brain research, morals, and culture. Breaking down these results gives a nuanced comprehension of the open doors and difficulties related with the powerful idea of reality transforming.

In the domain of innovation, the positive capability of reality transforming is obvious in applications that improve human encounters. Virtual and increased reality innovations, for example, offer vivid conditions that can be utilized for amusement, schooling, and remedial purposes. The positive outcome lies in the capacity of these advances to move people to recreated universes, giving chances to learning, expertise improvement, and profound prosperity.

Think about the utilization of augmented reality in training, where understudies can investigate verifiable occasions, take apart complex logical ideas, or participate in vivid language growth opportunities. The positive outcome is the potential for improved commitment and maintenance, as these innovations take special care of different learning styles and deal an experiential aspect to schooling.

In medical care, reality transforming advancements hold guarantee for restorative mediations. Augmented reality has been utilized to treat fears, post-awful pressure problem (PTSD), and agony the board. By making controlled, vivid conditions, these advancements offer a positive result by furnishing people with devices to face and defeat difficulties in a protected and controlled setting.

Be that as it may, the positive capability of reality transforming in innovation likewise brings moral contemplations. The obscuring of lines among virtual and actual real factors brings up issues about the potential for dependence, separation, or a reduced feeling of the real world. People connecting widely in virtual conditions might confront difficulties in recognizing the mimicked and the genuine, affecting their discernments and ways of behaving in the actual world.

One more sure outcome of reality transforming lies in the potential for upgraded correspondence and joint effort. Increased reality applications can work with far off joint effort by overlaying computerized data onto the actual climate. This can possibly change businesses like assembling, support, and medical services, where specialists can give direction or help from a distance, prompting expanded productivity and decreased costs.

In any case, the expanded mix of increased reality into day to day existence likewise raises worries about security and observation. The consistent overlay of computerized data on the actual world might bring about a deficiency of individual space and an increased feeling of reconnaissance. Finding some kind of harmony between the positive results of improved correspondence and coordinated effort and the expected unfortunate results of protection encroachment turns into a pivotal moral thought truly transforming innovations.

The mental component of reality transforming stretches out past innovation, enveloping the manners by which people see and build their own real factors. Positive outcomes incorporate the potential for mental upgrade and personal development. Neurotechnologies that expect to upgrade mental capabilities, for example, memory or consideration, offer open doors for people to improve their psychological capacities.

Then again, the quest for mental improvement brings up moral issues with respect to reasonableness, access, and cultural assumptions. Assuming specific people approach innovations that upgrade mental capacities, it might fuel existing imbalances and make a mental separation. Moral contemplations include guaranteeing impartial admittance to mental upgrade advancements and tending to the expected cultural ramifications of improved mental capacities.

The positive results of reality transforming in brain research likewise stretch out to remedial mediations. Progresses in neurofeedback and mind PC interfaces offer expected medicines for conditions like sorrow, tension, and neurological issues.

The capacity to adjust cerebrum movement and give continuous criticism has groundbreaking ramifications for emotional wellness treatment.

Nonetheless, the moral contemplations in involving neurotechnologies for emotional well-being treatment include issues of assent, security, and the potential for unseen side-effects. The almost negligible difference between remedial mediations and obtrusive control of mental states requires cautious moral examination to guarantee that people are engaged in their emotional well-being ventures without undermining their independence.

Social and cultural stories are significantly impacted by reality transforming, with both positive and unfortunate results. Positive results incorporate the democratization of narrating and the intensification of different voices. Computerized stages give people the resources to share their accounts, viewpoints, and encounters on a worldwide scale, cultivating a more comprehensive portrayal of social variety.

Be that as it may, the positive capability of reality transforming in social stories likewise raises worries about falsehood and the spread of destructive philosophies. The straightforwardness with which data can be controlled or mutilated in the computerized age presents difficulties to the validness of accounts. The adverse result includes the potential for the spread of misleading data, the making of protected, closed off environments, and the disintegration of confidence in shared real factors.

The positive results of reality transforming in social stories additionally stretch out to the potential for social change and activism. Computerized stages give a strong medium to minimized voices to challenge predominant stories, prepare networks, and promoter for civil rights. The capacity to reshape social stories has extraordinary ramifications for developments resolving issues like imbalance, separation, and common freedoms.

Nonetheless, the positive potential for social change through reality transforming likewise faces difficulties like algorithmic predisposition and online control. The calculations that curate content on computerized stages may coincidentally support existing inclinations or focus on dramatist content. Moral contemplations include addressing these predispositions to guarantee that reality transforming contributes decidedly to social change without sustaining imbalances or encouraging division.

The monetary ramifications of reality transforming are complex, with positive outcomes like development, effectiveness, and new open doors coinciding with potential adverse results like work relocation and financial disparity. In businesses, for example, fabricating, the combination of expanded reality and man-made consciousness can prompt more proficient creation processes, diminished mistakes, and worked on in general efficiency.

Notwithstanding, the positive results of expanded proficiency through reality transforming innovations additionally raise worries about work relocation and the requirement for reskilling the labor force. The potential for robotization to supplant specific assignments might bring about monetary abberations in the event that not joined by extensive techniques for labor force change and ability advancement.

The positive potential for business and financial development is additionally clear in the improvement of reality transforming advancements. New businesses and pioneers investigating increased reality, augmented reality, and other transforming advancements add to monetary dynamism and the making of new business sectors.

This positive result lines up with the potential for mechanical headways to drive monetary advancement.

Be that as it may, the financial ramifications of reality transforming likewise incorporate the convergence of force among tech goliaths and worries about monopolistic practices. The predominance of a couple of significant organizations in the turn of events and control of reality transforming innovations brings up moral issues about rivalry, market access, and the impartial circulation of financial advantages.

Moral contemplations in the domain of reality transforming stretch out to the potential for abuse and unseen side-effects. The positive outcomes of reality transforming advances, like customized encounters and upgraded abilities, might be taken advantage of for malevolent purposes. Deepfake innovation, for instance, can possibly control media content and make persuading yet misleading portrayals of people, prompting deception, data fraud, or notoriety harm.

Security and protection concerns additionally arise as critical moral contemplations. The mix of reality transforming advances into day to day existence, from brilliant homes to wearable gadgets, brings up issues about the security of individual information, reconnaissance, and the potential for unapproved access. Guaranteeing strong network protection measures and security shields becomes essential in relieving the unfortunate results related with reality transforming.

All in all, reality transforming presents a range of potential outcomes that length mechanical, mental, social, financial, and moral aspects. The positive outcomes incorporate upgraded encounters, remedial intercessions, democratized narrating, and financial open doors. Notwithstanding, these positive perspectives exist together with adverse results, for example, moral problems, security concerns, cultural imbalances, and the potential for abuse.

Exploring the moral contemplations of reality transforming requires a multidisciplinary approach that includes joint effort between technologists, clinicians, ethicists, policymakers, and society.

Reality transforming, with its capability to reshape discernments, encounters, and cultural stories, presents a horde of unfortunate results that length mechanical, mental, moral, and cultural aspects. As reality transforming innovations develop and turn out to be progressively coordinated into different parts of day to day existence, it is urgent to fundamentally look at the potential drawbacks related with these headways.

One noticeable unfortunate result of reality transforming lies in the moral ramifications of controlling data and contorting reality. Deepfake innovation, for example, empowers the making of sensible yet totally manufactured content, including recordings and sound accounts. The pernicious utilization of deepfakes presents serious dangers to people's notorieties, protection, and, surprisingly, public safety. Pantomime, deception, and the formation of misleading accounts can have extreme outcomes, dissolving trust in media and subverting the actual underpinnings of the real world.

The ascent of deepfakes raises worries about the potential for deception to be weaponized in different settings, from political missions to corporate damage. The conscious spread of misleading accounts through controlled media content can possibly impact popular assessment, influence decisions, and make confusion. This unfortunate result highlights the direness of creating strong location systems and administrative structures to battle the destructive impacts of falsehood worked with by reality transforming advancements.

Protection attack is one more huge adverse result related with reality transforming. As advancements like expanded reality, augmented reality, and reconnaissance frameworks become more refined, the limits among public and confidential spaces obscure. People might wind up accidentally exposed to reconnaissance or unapproved recording, encroaching upon their right to security. The abuse of reality transforming innovations for voyeuristic or malevolent purposes represents a serious danger to people's independence and individual security.

The incorporation of reality transforming into ordinary gadgets, like brilliant home frameworks and wearable innovations, enhances the potential for meddlesome observation. Consistent checking and information assortment raise worries about the unapproved utilization of individual data, prompting potential fraud, profiling, and the control of standards of conduct. Defending protection in the time of reality transforming requires powerful legitimate systems, secure advances, and an elevated consciousness of the possible dangers.

One of the adverse results of reality transforming is the worsening of cultural divisions and the formation of protected, closed off environments. Calculations that curate customized content in light of people's inclinations can unintentionally add to the polarization of society. Clients might be presented fundamentally to data that lines up with their current convictions, building up previous inclinations and restricting openness to different viewpoints. This protected, closed off environment impact has suggestions for the working of majority rules systems, as people become dug in their perspectives and are less open to elective perspectives.

The unfortunate results of closed quarters stretch out past political polarization to social, social, and financial domains. Online people group that build up outrageous philosophies or oppressive convictions might add to the underestimation of specific gatherings. The fracture of cultural accounts hampers useful exchange and aggregate critical thinking, encouraging a climate where falsehood and disruptive stories flourish.

The mental effect of reality transforming acquaints unfortunate results related with psychological wellness and prosperity. The steady openness to changed or increased real factors, particularly through vivid innovations, may add to a feeling of separation from the actual world. People submerged in virtual conditions might encounter an obscuring of limits among the real world and reenactment, prompting difficulties in recognizing the two.

The unfortunate results of drawn out commitment with virtual or expanded real factors incorporate likely dependence, social seclusion, and a lessened feeling of presence in the actual world. Getting away into vivid encounters might give transitory help, however it brings up issues about the drawn out influence on people's psychological wellness and their capacity to explore genuine difficulties. Moral contemplations in the turn of events and arrangement of reality transforming advancements should focus on the prosperity of people and address likely pessimistic mental outcomes.

Reality transforming additionally presents pessimistic results in the domain of relational connections. The expanded dependence on computerized correspondence and virtual collaborations might prompt a decrease in up close and personal social communications. As people submerge themselves in virtual universes or arranged web-based spaces, the profundity and legitimacy of human associations might lessen. The unfortunate result includes the likely disintegration of certified social securities, sympathy, and the subtleties of non-verbal correspondence.

In addition, reality transforming advancements can add to the commodification of individual connections. Web-based entertainment stages, specifically, frequently focus on measurements like preferences, offers, and supporters, making a quantifiable proportion of social approval. This evaluation of connections can prompt an unfortunate result where people focus on web-based prominence over significant associations, cultivating a culture of shallow communications and a twisted identity worth.

The unfortunate results of reality transforming are apparent in the potential for monetary disparity and occupation dislodging. While these advances offer open doors for development and productivity, the robotization of specific errands and the mix of man-made brainpower might bring about employment cutback for specific areas of the labor force. The unfortunate result includes the likely worsening of existing monetary variations, making a split between the people who have what it takes expected in a reality-transformed economy and the individuals who don't.

The uprooting of occupations by reality transforming advances brings up moral issues about cultural obligation and the requirement for proactive measures to address labor force changes. Drives, for example, reskilling programs, training changes, and extensive social strategies become vital in relieving the adverse results of financial disparity related with the coordination of reality transforming advancements.

The adverse results of reality transforming stretch out to the domain of social safeguarding and legitimacy. As expanded reality and computer generated reality encounters offer better approaches for drawing in with social legacy, there is a gamble of commodifying and weakening the meaning of social relics. The replication of verifiable locales, craftsmanships, or customary practices in virtual conditions might add to a shallow comprehension of social legacy, sabotaging the credibility and setting that make these components significant.

Besides, the adverse results of reality transforming in social safeguarding incorporate the potential for social appointment and the contortion of accounts. The deception of social characters in virtual spaces or the utilization of expanded reality for business gain might prompt the eradication of nuanced social stories and the propagation of hurtful generalizations. Moral contemplations truly transforming should focus on the conscious portrayal and conservation of assorted social legacy.

In the legitimate and moral area, the adverse results of reality transforming raise difficulties connected with responsibility, obligation, and the meaning of truth. Deepfakes, for instance, can be utilized to make created proof, bringing up issues about the unwavering quality of varying media materials in judicial procedures. The adverse result includes the expected control of proof, compromising the uprightness of the equity framework and prompting unfair allegations or exonerations.

The unfortunate results of reality transforming advances in the legitimate domain likewise reach out to issues of assent and computerized character. The unapproved utilization of people's similarity or voice in controlled media content stances difficulties to assent and brings up moral issues about the potential for data fraud. Legitimate systems should develop to address these moves and give roads to people to safeguard their advanced characters.

Chapter 9

The Future of Morphing Minds

In the tremendous scene of mechanical headway, what's to come holds the commitment of extraordinary changes that will alter the manner in which we see and cooperate with the world. At the very front of this development is the idea of transforming minds, a combination of neuroscience, man-made brainpower, and human increase that can possibly reshape the actual pith of human discernment and cognizance.

The approach of neurotechnology has prepared for extraordinary bits of knowledge into the functions of the human cerebrum. As how we might interpret brain processes extends, the potential outcomes of controlling and improving mental capabilities become progressively unmistakable. The cooperative energy among neuroscience and man-made reasoning is turning into a strong impetus for opening the maximum capacity of the human brain.

One of the critical components in store for transforming minds is cerebrum PC interface (BCI) innovation. BCIs overcome any barrier between the human cerebrum and outside gadgets, empowering an immediate line of correspondence between the psyche and machines. This has significant ramifications for people with handicaps, permitting them to control prosthetic appendages or associate with PCs utilizing only their considerations. Be that as it may, the extent of BCIs stretches out past healing applications, venturing into the domain of mental expansion.

Envision an existence where learning another dialect or getting an expertise is at this point not a tedious interaction. With cutting edge BCIs, data could be straightforwardly moved to the mind, bypassing customary techniques for schooling. The speed and productivity of learning would be unrivaled, introducing a time of uncommon information procurement and ability advancement.

The joining of man-made consciousness (artificial intelligence) into the transforming minds scene intensifies the extraordinary capability of these innovations. AI calculations can investigate immense measures of brain information, recognizing examples and connections that human cerebrums could disregard. This makes the way for customized mental upgrade, where simulated intelligence calculations tailor intercessions to the remarkable brain engineering of every person.

Moral contemplations pose a potential threat in the domain of transforming minds. The possibility of controlling or upgrading mental capabilities brings up issues about independence, assent, and the actual idea of being human. Finding some kind of harmony among progress and moral limits will be a characterizing challenge as we explore the unfamiliar regions of psyche increase.

Protection is another squeezing concern. As BCIs become more modern, the potential for unapproved admittance to people's viewpoints and encounters turns into a reality. Defending the sacredness of the brain will require powerful safety efforts and moral systems that focus on the prosperity of people over the quest for innovative progression.

The combination of transforming minds and computer generated reality (VR) acquaints another aspect with human experience. Envision having the option to drench yourself in a virtual world through sight and sound as well as through direct brain collaboration completely. This opens up opportunities for shared virtual encounters, clairvoyant correspondence, and the obscuring of limits between the physical and computerized domains.

As the limits among human and machine obscure, inquiries regarding personality and awareness come to the very front. What's the significance here to be human when our considerations and encounters can be expanded or even imparted to machines? The actual embodiment of awareness is raised doubt about as we investigate the strange regions of transforming minds.

Brain adaptability, the cerebrum's capacity to redesign and adjust, turns into a focal subject coming soon for transforming minds. As we gain the capacity to shape and reshape brain associations, the idea of a fixed and constant self becomes out of date. The flexibility of the psyche opens up opportunities for personal growth, self-awareness, and, surprisingly, the redefinition of one's own character.

Schooling goes through an extreme change in reality as we know it where transforming minds are the standard. The conventional model of homerooms and course books gives way to a dynamic and customized growth opportunity. Understudies can tailor their instructive excursions in light of their singular learning styles, interests, and mental qualities. The job of educators develops from disseminators of data to facilitators of the growing experience, directing understudies on their remarkable ways of information obtaining.

The working environment, as well, encounters a seismic shift. The abilities and information that were once the groundwork of expert achievement might become obsolete as the speed of mechanical headway speeds up. Versatility and an eagerness to embrace consistent learning become fundamental qualities in a labor force where transforming minds are plausible as well as a reality.

The potential for mental upgrade brings up issues about cultural value. Will admittance to mind-changing innovations be restricted to the special minority, making a mental split between the improved and the non-upgraded? Taking a stab at inclusivity and guaranteeing that the advantages of transforming minds are open to all turns into a critical part of molding a future that isn't defaced by disparity.

Clinical utilizations of transforming minds offer new roads for treating emotional wellness problems. Neurological circumstances, like gloom, nervousness, and PTSD, could be focused on at the brain level, giving more successful and customized medicines. In any case, the moral ramifications of utilizing these advances to change or improve state of mind and character bring up complex issues about the idea of human affliction and the limits of clinical mediation.

The idea of a collective conscience, where people are interconnected at the brain level, challenges our thoughts of independence. In this present reality where considerations can be shared quickly, the limits among self and others become liquid. The potential for aggregate critical thinking, shared encounters, and a profound feeling of interconnectedness opens up another boondocks in human social elements.

Legitimate systems fall behind innovative progressions, and the future of transforming minds is no exemption. Inquiries concerning responsibility for information, assent for mental mediations, and the meaning of mental freedoms become focal issues in the lawful scene. As we reclassify having organization over our viewpoints and encounters, the general set of laws should adjust to defend individual freedoms despite phenomenal innovative abilities.

The investigation of modified conditions of cognizance takes on new importance in this present reality where transforming minds is a reality. The utilization of neurotechnologies to initiate modified states, improve imagination, or even reproduce specific encounters prompts a reexamination of our cultural mentalities toward cognizance modifying substances. The line among normal and increased conditions of awareness obscures, testing assumptions about modified impression of the real world.

The crossing point of transforming psyches and imagination opens up opportunities for phenomenal creative articulation. Envision a painter who can decipher the feelings and dreams to them straightforwardly onto a material or a performer who can form ensembles by coordinating brain motivations. The combination of human imagination and mechanical expansion introduces another time of creative advancement and articulation.

Otherworldliness and the idea of the spirit go through a significant change with regards to transforming minds. As we unwind the secrets of cognizance and investigate the constraints of mental upgrade, conventional ideas of the spirit as a permanent and otherworldly element might give way to a more liquid and interconnected comprehension of profound presence.

The coordination of transforming minds with natural supportability presents additional opportunities for understanding and tending to worldwide difficulties.

The elevated mental capacities of upgraded people might add to creative answers for environmental change, asset exhaustion, and other major problems. In any case, the moral ramifications of utilizing mental upgrade to resolve cultural issues bring up complex issues about the crossing point of innovation, morals, and everyone's benefit.

As we stand on the slope representing things to come of transforming minds, the way ahead is full of moral, social, and existential difficulties. Our decisions today will shape the direction of human development in manners that were once the domain of sci-fi. Adjusting the expected advantages of mental improvement with the moral contemplations and cultural ramifications is a fragile dance that requires smart reflection and worldwide joint effort.

The future of transforming minds is a boondocks of vast conceivable outcomes and unfamiliar regions. It moves us to reexamine the actual idea of human life, awareness, and character. As we explore this neglected scene, the choices we cause will to characterize the eventual fate of innovation as well as the fate of humankind itself. The excursion into the transforming minds period is an odyssey that coaxes us to investigate the restrictions of our creative mind and the profundities of how we might interpret being human.

9.1 Speculate on the future of mind morphing and reality shaping

In the consistently developing scene of mechanical headways, what's to come holds the enticing possibility of psyche transforming and reality molding. As we dive into the domains of neuroscience, man-made brainpower, and expanded reality, we start to witness a future where the limits between the psyche and outer reality obscure in phenomenal ways.

At the core of this hypothesis is the idea of psyche transforming - the capacity to change and upgrade mental capabilities through the mix of trend setting innovations with the human cerebrum. This could introduce a time where our extremely perspectives are increased, prompting new elements of imagination, critical thinking, and self-improvement. Simultaneously, the possibility of reality molding imagines an existence where our impression of the outside climate are pliable, impacted by the actual world as well as by expanded and computer generated realities.

One of the critical advances driving this hypothesis is neurotechnology, especially cerebrum PC interfaces (BCIs). These connection points lay out an immediate connection between the human cerebrum and outer gadgets, opening up potential outcomes that were once restricted to the domains of sci-fi. The capacity to disentangle and decipher brain signals holds the way to opening the maximum capacity of psyche transforming, permitting us to improve mental capacities and reshape the manner in which we see and collaborate with the world.

As we peer into the future, one of the most charming possibilities is the possibility of mental increase. Envision an existence where people can upgrade their memory, mental speed, and critical thinking abilities through brain intercessions. High level BCIs could work with the immediate exchange of data into the cerebrum, speeding up the educational experience and extending the restrictions of human knowledge. This has significant ramifications for schooling, proficient turn of events, and the actual structure holding the system together.

Notwithstanding, the way to mental expansion is overflowing with moral contemplations. Inquiries regarding the meaning of human personality, the potential for making mental incongruities, and the ramifications of controlling the actual substance of thought request cautious investigation. Finding some kind of harmony between the craving for mental upgrade and the moral limits that shield individual independence turns into a principal challenge in the speculative scene of brain transforming.

Reality forming, then again, reaches out past the bounds of the brain to envelop the outer climate. Expanded reality (AR) and computer generated reality (VR) innovations are ready to assume a focal part in this theoretical future. AR overlays computerized data onto the actual world, while VR submerges people in totally engineered conditions. The intermingling of these advancements holds the possibility to reshape our view of reality itself.

Envision an existence where people can consistently progress among physical and virtual spaces, where the limits between the genuine and the reenacted become liquid. This could lead to another period of experiential diversion, vivid instruction, and novel types of correspondence. Virtual gatherings could rise above the limits of actual distance, permitting people to connect in shared virtual spaces as though they were in a similar room.

The reconciliation of brain transforming and reality forming innovations presents the idea of "brain reality." In this speculative future, our mental cycles straightforwardly communicate with expanded and computer generated realities, making a harmonious connection between the psyche and the computerized domain. The ramifications of this combination stretch out past simple amusement and correspondence, affecting the manner in which we work, learn, and see our general surroundings.

Moral contemplations reverberation in the domain of reality forming also. The potential for controlling discernments and bringing up engineered conditions raises doubts about the genuineness of encounters and the effect on mental prosperity. Finding some kind of harmony between the advantages of expanded and computer generated realities and the possible dangers of separation from the actual world turns into a basic part of forming a capable future.

The speculative scene additionally presents the thought of shared brain encounters. Imagine a scenario where people couldn't see expanded or computer generated realities separately yet additionally share their encounters straightforwardly at the brain level. This idea rises above customary types of correspondence, preparing for a shared perspective where contemplations, feelings, and encounters are partaken in manners beforehand unfathomable.

The possibility of a common brain experience difficulties customary thoughts of security and singularity. As we mull over a future where the limits between minds become permeable, questions emerge about assent, individual space, and the ramifications of shared brain network. Exploring the moral elements of shared brain encounters turns into an intricate undertaking, requiring a nuanced comprehension of the convergence among innovation and human qualities.

The joining of psyche transforming and reality molding advancements likewise raises worries about security and control. The potential for unapproved admittance to brain information, control of mental cycles, and the production of manufactured encounters without assent highlight the requirement for hearty safety efforts and moral rules. Protecting the respectability of the psyche and the genuineness of individual encounters turns into a basic in the speculative future.

The instructive scene goes through a change in perspective in this present reality where brain transforming and reality molding are universal. Conventional homerooms might give way to vivid learning conditions, where understudies draw in with instructive substance through direct brain interfaces.

The capacity to reenact authentic occasions, direct virtual examinations, and investigate conceptual ideas in three-layered brain reality could change the manner we approach schooling.

Essentially, the work environment changes into a dynamic and versatile climate. Far off cooperation takes on another aspect as people communicate in shared brain spaces, rising above the constraints of actual distance. The idea of work itself goes through a transformation, with the accentuation moving from routine undertakings to inventive critical thinking and imaginative reasoning. The interest for mental adaptability and flexibility becomes vital in a labor force where the limits between the natural and the fake haze.

The speculative fate of psyche transforming and reality forming additionally allures us to reexamine how we might interpret cognizance. As we investigate the outskirts of brain increase and shared encounters, basic inquiries concerning the idea of cognizance, emotional reality, and oneself come to the front. The actual embodiment of being cognizant in reality as we know it where psyches are transformed and truths are molded turns into a philosophical request that rises above mechanical contemplations.

The ramifications of psyche transforming and reality forming reach out past the individual and cultural levels to envelop more extensive worldwide difficulties. The increased mental capacities worked with by these advances might add to creative answers for complex issues, for example, environmental change, asset exhaustion, and general wellbeing emergencies. The convergence of mental expansion and worldwide difficulties prompts a reexamination of the job of improved people in resolving the major problems within recent memory.

Legitimate systems battle to stay up with the fast progressions as a primary concern transforming and reality molding innovations. Inquiries regarding responsibility for information, the right to mental protection, and the guideline of increased and augmented realities become vital to the legitimate talk. Making regulation that adjusts the likely advantages of these innovations with the need to safeguard individual freedoms and cultural prosperity represents an impressive test for legitimate specialists and policymakers.

As we adventure into the speculative eventual fate of brain transforming and reality forming, moving toward these potential outcomes with an insightful and moral mindset is critical. Our decisions in the turn of events and execution of these advancements will shape the direction of human development and the idea of our relationship with the computerized domain. Adjusting the craving for progress with the obligation to explore the moral elements of mental expansion and modified real factors turns into an aggregate undertaking that requires worldwide joint effort and reflection.

All in all, the eventual fate of psyche transforming and reality forming holds the commitment of an extraordinary time where the limits between the natural and the counterfeit, the brain and the outer climate, become progressively permeable.

The intermingling of neurotechnology, man-made reasoning, and increased reality opens up extraordinary opportunities for improving mental capabilities and reshaping our impression of the real world. Nonetheless, this theoretical future additionally presents significant moral, cultural, and existential difficulties that request cautious thought and mindful independent direction. As we explore this unknown region, the decisions today will characterize the idea of our future presence, obscuring the lines between what is genuine, what is envisioned, and what is yet to be found.

9.2 Discuss emerging technologies and their potential impact on consciousness

As we stand at the crossing point of mechanical development and human experience, the scene of arising innovations presents a horde of conceivable outcomes that reach out past the substantial domain of contraptions and gadgets. One of the significant areas of investigation is the expected effect of these advances on cognizance - the actual substance of our mindfulness, contemplations, and emotional encounters. In this talk, we dig into the diverse manners by which arising advances might impact and reshape cognizance.

Neurotechnology, especially progressions in mind PC interfaces (BCIs), stands apart as a wilderness with significant ramifications for cognizance. BCIs lay out an immediate connection between the human mind and outside gadgets, considering bidirectional correspondence. The potential for deciphering and deciphering brain signals opens up new roads for understanding and, somewhat, controlling cognizance.

The idea of brain interfaces prompts hypothesis about the increase of human mental capacities. Envision a future where people can improve their memory, handling velocity, or even procure new abilities straightforwardly through brain intercessions. BCIs could work with the exchange of data into the mind, speeding up the educational experience and extending the constraints of mental capacities. This raises moral contemplations about the idea of human personality, independence, and the likely cultural ramifications of mental differences.

Besides, neurotechnology opens ways to the investigation of changed conditions of awareness. By interacting with brain processes, it becomes possible to actuate explicit mental states or even reenact encounters that rise above the common. While this brings up moral issues about the mindful utilization of such advancements and the likely dangers of controlling awareness, it additionally presents the chance of remedial applications for psychological well-being problems or improving prosperity.

Man-made reasoning (simulated intelligence) assumes a critical part in the developing scene of arising advances. AI calculations, equipped for breaking down tremendous measures of information and recognizing complex examples, offer bits of knowledge into mental cycles and ways of behaving.

The collaboration among artificial intelligence and neuroscience opens up open doors for customized mental mediations, fitting encounters and increases to individual brain designs.

On the other hand, the coming of computer based intelligence controlled menial helpers and chatbots brings up issues about the idea of awareness in non-organic substances. As these advances become more refined in understanding and answering human feelings and subtleties, the line among machine and human awareness obscures. This prompts philosophical investigations into the pith of cognizance and the potential for fake elements to display types of mindfulness.

Increased reality (AR) and computer generated reality (VR) advances add to the developing account of awareness by changing the manner in which we see and collaborate with the world. AR overlays advanced data onto the actual climate, upgrading our tangible encounters, while VR drenches people in totally manufactured conditions. The combination of these innovations makes a blended reality where the limits between the genuine and the virtual become progressively liquid.

With regards to AR, the combination of computerized data into our regular insight brings up issues about the genuineness of our encounters. As our existence becomes expanded with extra layers of data, the qualification between what is veritable and what is carefully improved becomes obscured. This prompts reflections on the pliability of cognizance and the effect of increased real factors on our feeling of the real world.

VR, then again, offers a significant change of cognizance by shipping people to completely manufactured conditions. The vivid idea of VR encounters can possibly areas of strength for summon reactions and prompt a feeling of presence in virtual universes. This prompts examination about the idea of emotional reality and the manners by which virtual encounters might shape our discernments and cognizance.

The assembly of increased and computer generated realities brings about the idea of expanded reality (XR), where the limits among physical and advanced encounters disintegrate. In a XR scene, awareness isn't restricted to the constraints of the actual body yet stretches out into virtual domains. This presents novel open doors for shared encounters, cooperative imagination, and the investigation of modified conditions of awareness in virtual spaces.

The moral contemplations encompassing AR and VR advances are complex. Issues of assent, protection, and the possible mental effect of vivid encounters come to the front. As people draw in with expanded and computer generated realities, questions emerge about the drawn out consequences for emotional wellness, social elements, and the conservation of individual limits in our current reality where the qualification between the genuine and the reproduced is progressively nuanced.

The mix of vivid advances with virtual entertainment stages further enhances the likely effect on cognizance. Virtual social spaces, where people cooperate as symbols in shared advanced conditions, challenge conventional ideas of social connections. The ramifications for character, connections, and the development of online personas bring up issues about the realness of computerized associations and their impact on our healthy identity.

Blockchain innovation, initially created as the fundamental framework for digital currencies, presents novel opportunities for awareness with regards to character and possession. Blockchain's decentralized and straightforward nature considers the protected and undeniable capacity of individual information. This has suggestions for computerized character, where people have more prominent command over their own data, possibly affecting the manner in which we see and protect our personalities in the advanced domain.

The idea of decentralized independent associations (DAOs), empowered by blockchain innovation, presents another worldview for aggregate direction and administration. As people take part in these decentralized organizations, questions emerge about the idea of shared mindset and the potential for dispersed types of self-association. This difficulties conventional progressive designs and prompts reflections on the democratization of dynamic cycles.

The Web of Things (IoT), an organization of interconnected gadgets, adds to the developing story of cognizance by making a snare of universal network. Regular items implanted with sensors and availability become hubs in a huge organization, gathering and sharing information progressively. This interconnectedness prompts consideration about the manners by which our current circumstance, through savvy innovations, turns into an augmentation of our awareness.

The multiplication of IoT gadgets raises worries about protection and security. As our homes, working environments, and public spaces become immersed with interconnected innovations, the potential for reconnaissance and unapproved admittance to individual data turns into a major problem. This difficulties our ideas of security and prompts reflections on the compromises among accommodation and the assurance of individual independence.

Biotechnology, remembering propels for hereditary designing and engineered science, presents contemplations about the idea of awareness at the organic level. Hereditary intercessions might offer the possibility to alter mental capabilities, impact character qualities, or even location hereditary inclinations to specific emotional wellbeing conditions. While the moral ramifications of such intercessions are significant, they additionally open roads for investigating the hereditary premise of awareness.

The potential for fashioner children, where hereditary qualities related with insight or explicit gifts are chosen, prompts moral discussions about the idea of through and through freedom, variety, and the results of designing human characteristics.

The convergence of biotechnology and cognizance brings up issues about the embodiment of distinction and the moral limits of molding the organic groundworks of our mindfulness.

Quantum figuring, still in its outset yet progressing quickly, presents a change in outlook in computational power. Quantum PCs, utilizing the standards of quantum mechanics, can possibly take care of intricate issues at speeds out of reach by old style PCs. This has suggestions for how we might interpret cognizance with regards to computational models of the psyche.

The investigation of quantum cognizance, a hypothetical structure that recommends quantum peculiarities assume a part in mental cycles, builds up forward momentum with headways in quantum processing. The potential for quantum PCs to recreate and show parts of cognizance brings up issues about the connection between quantum mechanics and the secrets of mindfulness. Nonetheless, the speculative idea of quantum awareness additionally highlights the requirement for additional logical request and investigation.

The intermingling of these arising innovations makes an embroidery of potential outcomes that reach out past the domain of individual devices or logical disciplines. As we think about the likely effect on cognizance, it is fundamental to explore the moral, cultural, and philosophical aspects that go with these mechanical progressions. Finding some kind of harmony among development and obligation turns into a focal subject in molding a future where innovation expands human encounters without compromising the center components of our cognizance.

9.3 Explore the evolving understanding of the mind and its role in shaping the future

The investigation of the brain and its mind boggling functions has been a crucial part of human request since forever ago. As we stand on the incline of innovative progressions, neuroscience leap forwards, and philosophical reflections, how we might interpret the psyche is going through a significant development. In this investigation, we dig into the multi-layered components of the brain, its part in forming the future, and the transaction between innovation, cognizance, and cultural change.

The conventional comprehension of the brain as a static and segregated element is giving way to an additional dynamic and interconnected model. The rise of brain adaptability as a key idea highlights the mind's exceptional capacity to adjust and revamp itself in light of encounters, learning, and ecological boosts. This pliability challenges assumptions about the proper idea of the psyche and opens up opportunities for self-awareness, recovery, and, surprisingly, the redefinition of character.

Neuroscience, pushed by mechanical progressions in imaging and information examination, is unwinding the intricacies of the cerebrum with phenomenal accuracy. Practical Attractive Reverberation Imaging (fMRI), Electroencephalography (EEG), and other neuroimaging methods give experiences into brain processes, mental capabilities, and the brain associates of awareness. The marriage of neuroscience and innovation is encouraging a more profound comprehension of the psyche mind relationship and preparing for inventive mediations.

The combination of neuroscience and man-made consciousness (man-made intelligence) denotes a change in outlook in the investigation of the brain. AI calculations can investigate huge datasets, distinguishing examples and connections that might escape human perception. This advantageous connection among neuroscience and man-made intelligence improves our capacity to interpret the intricacies of discernment, anticipate brain reactions, and even mimic specific parts of mental cycles.

The ascent of cerebrum PC interfaces (BCIs) remains as a demonstration of the groundbreaking capability of consolidating innovation with the brain. BCIs lay out an immediate correspondence interface between the mind and outside gadgets, empowering a scope of utilizations from neuroprosthetics for people with inabilities to mental upgrades. The incorporation of BCIs with virtual and increased reality further grows the potential outcomes, taking into account direct brain cooperations with computerized conditions.

The advancing comprehension of the psyche stretches out past the person to envelop aggregate and disseminated types of discernment. The idea of the drawn out mind sets that mental cycles are not restricted to the limits of the skull however reach out into the outside climate and innovative antiquities. This difficulties the customary idea of an independent psyche and prompts thought about the manners by which outer instruments and innovations become basic to mental cycles.

As we explore this developing scene of the psyche, inquiries regarding the idea of cognizance come to the very front. The difficult issue of awareness, as expressed by scholar David Chalmers, digs into the secret of why and how emotional encounters emerge from brain processes. While logical headways shed light on the brain relates of cognizance, the substance of emotional mindfulness stays a philosophical and magical riddle.

The approach of computer generated reality (VR) and expanded reality (AR) acquaints novel aspects with the investigation of awareness. VR drenches people in totally engineered conditions, making a feeling of presence and commitment that challenges our view of the real world. AR overlays advanced data onto the actual world, obscuring the limits between the genuine and the virtual. The exchange between these vivid advancements and awareness brings up issues about the idea of insight, reality, and the effect of virtual encounters on our mental cycles.

The idea of counterfeit cognizance arises as a provocative investigation in the domain of simulated intelligence and mechanical technology. As machines become progressively modern in mirroring human ways of behaving, feelings, and, surprisingly, mindfulness, moral contemplations about the idea of fake cognizance come to the front. The potential for machines to display types of abstract experience prompts reflections on the ethical ramifications, cultural results, and the moral treatment of counterfeit substances.

Moral contemplations pose a potential threat in the developing comprehension of the psyche, especially as innovation becomes entwined with mental cycles. Inquiries regarding security, assent, and the dependable utilization of neurotechnologies highlight the requirement for moral systems that defend individual independence and prosperity. The potential for mind-understanding innovations, which can translate and decipher contemplations, raises complex moral issues about the limits among individual and brain protection.

The coordination of the brain and innovation additionally has significant ramifications for schooling. The customary model of training, with its accentuation on normalized educational programs and evaluation, is being tested by the acknowledgment of individual contrasts in learning styles and mental qualities. Customized learning, worked with by simulated intelligence calculations that adjust instructive substance to individual necessities, offers a brief look into a future where training is custom-made to the special mental profiles of every understudy.

The working environment goes through a change as the developing comprehension of the psyche illuminates hierarchical practices. The acknowledgment of mental variety prompts a shift from a one-size-fits-all way to deal with a more comprehensive and versatile workplace. The interest for abilities like capacity to understand people on a deeper level, imagination, and flexibility becomes vital in a labor force where mental upgrades, neurotechnologies, and man-made intelligence assume significant parts.

Cultural changes are not too far off as the advancing comprehension of the brain converges with more extensive worldwide difficulties. The acknowledgment of the interconnectedness of human personalities and the aggregate idea of comprehension prompts a reexamination of social designs, administration, and the manners by which we address shared issues. The potential for a more sympathetic and empathetic culture emerges as we extend how we might interpret the brain premise of sympathy and social association.

The investigation of changed conditions of cognizance takes on new aspects in reality as we know it where innovation and the psyche meet. The utilization of neurotechnologies to instigate modified states, improve inventiveness, or mimic specific encounters prompts a reconsideration of cultural perspectives toward cognizance changing substances. The line among normal and increased conditions of awareness obscures, testing assumptions about adjusted view of the real world and the idea of emotional encounters.

Lawful structures face moves in adjusting to the advancing comprehension of the brain and its joining with innovation. Inquiries concerning the responsibility for information, mental privileges, and the guideline of neurotechnologies become integral to lawful talk. Finding some kind of harmony between cultivating development and safeguarding individual privileges turns into a complicated undertaking, requiring legitimate specialists to explore the complexities of a quickly changing innovative scene.

As humankind tears into what was to come, impelled by a speeding up flood of mechanical headways, the job of innovation in forming our aggregate predetermination turns out to be progressively vital. This many-sided dance among advancement and cultural change entwines with different features of human life, addressing financial matters, training, medical care, correspondence, and the actual texture of social designs. In this investigation, we dig into the diverse manners by which innovation shapes our future, pondering its effect, challenges, and the obligations it offers to us.

Monetary Scene:

One of the most noticeable and significant impacts of innovation is obvious in the monetary scene. The ascent of mechanization, driven by man-made brainpower (simulated intelligence) and advanced mechanics, changes businesses and work markets. While computerization upgrades effectiveness and efficiency, it likewise raises worries about work dislodging and the requirement for reskilling the labor force. The fate of work is described by a powerful interchange among people and machines, where flexibility and the obtaining of new abilities become fundamental for proficient endurance and achievement.

Moreover, arising innovations add to the advancement of monetary models. Digital forms of money, empowered by blockchain innovation, challenge conventional monetary frameworks, offering decentralized and secure other options. The digitization of monetary standards, exemplified by ideas like National Bank Computerized Monetary forms (CBDCs), indicates a future where the idea of cash itself goes through basic changes. The ramifications for monetary incorporation, security, and the power elements inside the worldwide economy are huge contemplations as we explore this mechanical wilderness.

Instruction and Learning:

The domain of instruction goes through a change in perspective as innovation reclassifies customary models of learning. The digitization of instructive substance, the multiplication of web based learning stages, and the joining of man-made reasoning in customized opportunities for growth mark the development of a more adaptable and open instructive scene. The fate of schooling is described by a takeoff from normalized approaches, with a more noteworthy accentuation on versatile learning ways custommade to individual necessities and learning styles.

Virtual and increased reality innovations add another aspect to instructive encounters. Vivid reenactments and virtual homerooms rise above geological limits, offering understudies a different scope of learning conditions. The gamification of training, worked with by innovation, changes the growing experience into a drawing in and intuitive excursion. In any case, the computerized gap and difficulties connected with fair admittance to innovation stay basic issues that should be addressed to guarantee that the advantages of mechanical progressions in schooling are available to all.

Medical care Upheaval:

The crossing point of innovation and medical care is ready to upset the manner in which we approach clinical finding, therapy, and patient consideration. The approach of telemedicine extends admittance to medical care administrations, especially in remote or underserved regions. Wearable gadgets and wellbeing observing advancements give people ongoing experiences into their prosperity, empowering proactive wellbeing the executives. Computerized reasoning, with its capacity to examine immense datasets and distinguish designs, adds to symptomatic accuracy and the improvement of customized treatment plans.

Genomic medication, enabled by progressions in DNA sequencing advances, opens new wildernesses in understanding and treating hereditary problems. The potential for quality altering advances, like CRISPR, to change and address hereditary inconsistencies raises moral contemplations about the ramifications of controlling the human genome. As innovation keeps on reclassifying the potential outcomes inside medical care, the requirement for moral systems, information security, and the impartial dispersion of clinical progressions turns out to be progressively articulated.

Correspondence and Network:

Innovation has changed the manner in which we convey, associate, and offer data. The coming of the web, trailed by the multiplication of virtual entertainment stages, has made a worldwide interconnected society. The democratization of data, worked with by innovation, engages people to get to information, offer viewpoints, and partake in worldwide discussions. Nonetheless, the ascent of deception and the difficulties of exploring the advanced scene highlight the significance of computerized proficiency and mindful internet based ways of behaving.

The eventual fate of correspondence unfurls in a scene where arising advancements reclassify the potential outcomes of network. 5G innovation guarantees quicker and more dependable organizations, laying the preparation for the Web of Things (IoT) and the interconnectivity of savvy gadgets. The reconciliation of expanded reality (AR) and augmented reality (VR) into correspondence encounters offers vivid and intelligent methods of commitment. As innovation keeps on molding the manner in which we impart, saving security, cultivating inclusivity, and relieving the adverse consequence of advanced advances on mental prosperity become fundamental contemplations.

Cultural Effects:

The cultural effects of innovation are wide and significant, pervading each part of our day to day routines. Social designs go through changes as innovation impacts the manner in which we work, cooperate, and structure networks. The ascent of remote work, advanced by computerized network and cooperation instruments, challenges conventional thoughts of office-based business. The decentralization of workplaces brings up issues about urbanization, driving, and the conveyance of monetary open doors across locales.

Besides, the impact of innovation on cultural elements stretches out to issues of value and incorporation. The computerized partition, described by differences in admittance to innovation and advanced assets, compounds existing disparities. Overcoming this issue becomes basic to guarantee that the advantages of mechanical headways are open to all fragments of society. Furthermore, issues of algorithmic inclination, separation, and the moral utilization of computer based intelligence advancements require cautious thought and proactive measures to forestall the support of cultural disparities.

The job of innovation in molding what's to come is complicatedly attached to ecological manageability. The natural effect of innovative creation, energy utilization, and electronic waste administration raise worries about the biological impression of our mechanical progressions. The quest for green innovations, environmentally friendly power sources, and maintainable practices turns into a basic in creating a future where mechanical advancement coincides amicably with the planet.

Challenges and Moral Contemplations:

In the midst of the commitments and possibilities, the developing job of innovation in forming what's in store isn't without its difficulties and moral contemplations. Security arises as a focal worry as innovation works with the assortment, examination, and usage of huge measures of individual information. Finding some kind of harmony between the advantages of information driven experiences and the security of individual protection turns into a sensitive dance in the computerized age.

The moral components of man-made brainpower come to the very front as machines become more complex in dynamic cycles. Guaranteeing straightforwardness, responsibility, and decency in computer based intelligence calculations is basic to forestall one-sided results and unfair practices. Furthermore, the moral ramifications of independent frameworks, for example, self-driving vehicles and robots, request cautious thought to resolve inquiries of wellbeing, obligation, and cultural effect.

The moral utilization of biotechnologies, including quality altering and cloning, brings up significant issues about the limits of human mediation in the regular request. As we gain the capacity to control the basic structure blocks of life, moral systems should direct our choices to guarantee that the potential advantages are lined up with virtues and regard for the inborn pride of living creatures.

Obligation and Administration:

As innovation turns into a consistently present power molding the future, the subject of liability and administration becomes foremost. Mechanical progressions outperform the improvement of administrative structures, making a slack that presents dangers and difficulties. The requirement for spry and responsive administration models, both at the public and worldwide levels, is critical to guarantee that innovation serves humankind as opposed to compounding existing cultural issues.

Besides, encouraging a culture of moral advancement and dependable innovation improvement turns into a common obligation among innovation engineers, policymakers, and society at large. Moral contemplations should be coordinated into the plan and execution of advancements, expecting likely cultural effects and relieving gambles before they manifest. A cooperative and multidisciplinary approach, including specialists from different fields, is crucial for address the perplexing and interconnected difficulties presented by the developing job of innovation.

Conclusion

In the complex embroidered artwork of human life, the assembly of thought and reality frames the core of our aggregate insight. The complicated dance between our psyches and the substantial world we possess has been a subject of interminable interest and request. As we explore the maze of cognizance and the outside domain, the idea of transforming minds molding real factors arises as a significant investigation into the interaction of insight and the material world. This excursion takes us through the domains of brain research, reasoning, neuroscience, and then some, disentangling the powerful powers that weave the texture of our discernments, convictions, and the actual idea of reality itself.

At the core of the matter lies the crucial inquiry: How much do our psyches impact and shape the real factors we see? This request leads us down a diverse way where the flexibility of the brain meets with the inflexibility of the outside world. The idea of transforming minds exemplifies the groundbreaking power inserted inside human cognizance, rising above the limits of customary reasoning to form the shapes of our lived encounters.

One of the critical fields in which the transforming of psyches applies its impact is in the domain of discernment. The brain fills in as a refined channel through which we decipher and figure out the outer boosts besieging our faculties. Through this perplexing system, the brain gets data as well as effectively takes part in building the apparent reality. From the notable work of Gestalt clinicians to the cutting edge comprehension of perceptual steadiness, we unwind the many-sided systems through which our psyches transform divided sensations into rational and significant wholes.

Discernment, be that as it may, is definitely not a uninvolved demonstration. It is a functioning development, molded by mental cycles that are dependent upon a bunch of inside and outside factors. The exchange between hierarchical handling, impacted by earlier information and assumptions, and base up handling, driven by crude tangible information, highlights the multifaceted dance of transforming minds in forming the real factors we possess. As we explore the perplexing scene of insight, we come to see the value in the unique idea of our mental contraption, equipped for twisting, extending, and transforming the crude information of the outside world into the embroidered artwork of our abstract insight.

The pliability of discernment reaches out past the prompt tactile information sources and dives into the domain of memory. Memory, that subtle workforce that winds around together the strings of our previous encounters, is a dynamic and reconstructive cycle.

The transforming of brains is obvious in the specific encoding, stockpiling, and recovery of recollections, where the actual demonstration of memory turns into an imaginative undertaking as opposed to a reliable multiplication of previous occasions. The uncertainty of memory, as featured by mental analysts and neuroscientists the same, highlights the groundbreaking force of the psyche in forming our own stories.

In addition, the impact of culture, language, and cultural standards further emphasizes the versatility of our mental scene. The transforming of brains inside the more extensive setting of social systems appears in the molding of aggregate real factors. From Sapir-Whorf's etymological relativity speculation to the social brain science points of view supported by researchers, for example, Richard Shweder and Geert Hofstede, we witness the significant effect of social powers on molding individual insights as well as the actual texture of shared real factors. The transforming psyches of a general public all in all add to the development of standards, values, and conviction frameworks that, thus, shape the lived encounters of its individuals.

As we navigate the scene of transforming minds, the excursion dives further into the brain substrates of cognizance. The blossoming area of neuroscience gives uncommon experiences into the unpredictable dance among cerebrum and brain. The pliancy of the cerebrum, when remembered to be bound to early formative stages, is presently perceived as a long lasting peculiarity. Brain adaptability, the capacity of the cerebrum to redesign itself because of involvement, frames a foundation in understanding how the transforming psyches of people adjust to new difficulties, learn, and explore the intricacies of the consistently evolving reality.

The crossing point of neuroscience and innovation opens up new wildernesses in the investigation of transforming minds. Cerebrum PC interfaces, neurofeedback, and progressions in neuroimaging advances enable us to test the profundities of the psyche with uncommon accuracy. As we stand at the cliff of these mechanical progressions, moral contemplations pose a potential threat, enticing us to proceed cautiously in our mission to comprehend and control the actual pith of cognizance. The transforming minds in the time of neurotechnology suggest significant conversation starters about the limits of security, organization, and the moral ramifications of connecting with the brain substrates of our viewpoints and discernments.

Philosophical reflections on the idea of the real world and the brain have been a lasting undertaking that rises above social and fleeting limits. From antiquated Eastern methods of reasoning to Western existentialism, the talk on the connection among brain and reality reverberations through the halls of human scholarly history. The insights of savants like Immanuel Kant, who placed the possibility that the psyche effectively structures our experience of the real world, reverberate with contemporary understandings of the transforming minds forming the shapes of our emotional universes.

Amidst these philosophical requests, the idea of cognizance arises as a key part interfacing the domains of brain and reality. The tricky idea of cognizance, frequently compared to a "difficult issue" by rationalists like David Chalmers, stays a boondocks where the transforming psyches of researchers, savants, and scholars combine in their endeavors to disentangle the mystery. Hypotheses going from panpsychism to coordinated data hypothesis offer different points of view on how awareness emerges and, thusly, shapes our misgiving of the real world. The complex dance between the abstract insight of cognizance and the objective reality we see shapes an existential woven artwork that keeps on enrapturing the human keenness.

The transforming minds forming real factors reach out past the individual and aggregate human experience to envelop the more extensive natural and planetary setting. The interconnectedness of every single living framework, as elucidated by scientists, frameworks scholars, and ecological rationalists, highlights the cooperative connection between the human psyche and the environments we occupy. The biological emergency of our times fills in as a distinct sign of the results of disregarding the many-sided dance between our mental cycles and the unmistakable world. The transforming brains of people and social orders assume a crucial part in forming natural mentalities, ways of behaving, and strategies that, thus, impact the unfurling truth of our common planetary home.

In the computerized age, the transforming minds story takes on new aspects as we wrestle with the effect of data advances on our mental scenes. The universality of online entertainment, the coming of computer generated reality, and the fast dispersal of data reshape the manner in which we see, associate, and get a handle on the world. The computerized domain turns into a jungle gym where the transforming psyches of people are impacted by as well as effectively take part in forming the stories that penetrate the virtual space. The subject of computerized character, the obscuring of on the web and disconnected real factors, and the cultural ramifications of the advanced age enhance the intricacies of the transforming minds account in the 21st 100 years.

As we ponder the far reaching landscape of transforming minds molding real factors, it becomes clear that this investigation rises above disciplinary limits. The combination of brain research, neuroscience, reasoning, humanism, nature, and innovation shapes a rich embroidery that welcomes us to mull over the complex dance among psyche and reality from different vantage focuses. This multi-faceted point of view highlights the interconnectedness of apparently divergent strings in our mission to understand the idea of cognizance and the unique powers that form our discernments, convictions, and lived encounters.